HERBS FO̶ ̶ ̶
AND R̶ ̶ ̶ ̶ ̶ ̶
 a beginner's guide

TERESA MOOREY

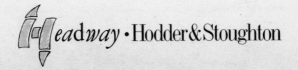

The author and publishers would like to thank Sean Knight from the Church of All
Worlds in Australia for providing information for this book.

Illustrations by Jane Brideson

Orders: please contact Bookpoint Ltd, 39 Milton Park, Abingdon, Oxon OX14 4TD.
Telephone: (44) 01235 400414, Fax: (44) 01235 400454. Lines are open from
9.00–6.00, Monday to Saturday, with a 24 hour message answering service. Email
address: orders@bookpoint.co.uk

British Library Cataloguing in Publication Data
A catalogue record for this title is available from The British Library

ISBN 0 340 674156

First published 1996
Impression number   12 11 10 9 8 7 6 5 4 3
Year   2004 2003 2002 2001 2000 1999 1998

Copyright © 1996 Teresa Moorey

Typeset by Transet Limited, Coventry, England.
Printed in Great Britain for Hodder & Stoughton Educational, a division of Hodder
Headline Plc, 338 Euston Road, London NW1 3BH by Cox & Wyman Ltd,
Reading, Berks.

CONTENTS

INTRODUCTION

*To you the earth yields her fruit, and you shall not want if
you but know how to fill your hands*

Kahlil Gibran *The Prophet*

This is a short book about a vast subject. For herbs are 'useful
plants' and that covers almost everything that grows on the wide
Earth. Some plants serve us as food and flavouring, some for
medicine or scent. Trees offer us wood for countless purposes. Even
poisonous plants are fascinating, and everything is notable for its
sheer beauty, from the humble blade of grass to the majestic oak.
Plants have magical uses too. Each living thing has its own
signature, its own special powers, and if we take the trouble to tune
in to this the magic of herbs can be ours.

In these pages you will find an introduction to the meaning and
mystery of herbs. This is only the beginning of a quest. Explore
further for yourself, experiment, grow plants, touch them, try out oils
and incenses and see what they mean to you – play with herbs for
the fun of it. Contact with these gifts of Nature is life-enhancing in
itself.

Humble, wise, mysterious and ancient, yet so accessible, herbs grow
in the footprints of the Goddess. Contact with them can be an act of
worship, or it can be just an interesting and creative pastime.
Discover for yourself.

MAGIC AND MEANINGS

Definition: Magic is the practice of causing change through the use of powers as yet not defined or accepted by science.

... Magic is knowledge – not only of its ways and laws, but also of its effectiveness. Do not believe that magic works – KNOW IT!

Scott Cunningham, *Cunningham's Encyclopedia of Magical Herbs*

As this book is largely about the magical use of herbs, there are certain concepts that we need to consider before we concentrate on the herbs themselves. This chapter offers a brief discussion of magic, its philosophy and certain practices, where it is particularly relevant to the use of herbs.

What is magic?

The most popular definition of magic at the moment seems to be 'the art of changing consciousness at will'. It may be all too easy, however, with this definition in mind, to dismiss magic as self-delusion. Of course, working magic can involve self-delusion, and that is something that all practitioners need to bear in mind, for there is a fine – but significant – line between delusion and creative use of the imagination. The power of belief is certainly part of

working magic, although this sort of belief is better called 'inner knowledge'. However, there is rather more to it than that.

Changing our consciousness is no small thing. We are apt to believe that our perception of the Universe is 'real' and down-to-earth people stress the importance of what they apprehend with their five senses. This attitude is upheld by a materialistic culture. However, our impression of the world around us is a construct of the brain. It would be more 'real' to regard the solid desk where I sit as an energy centre, a localised disturbance in some cosmic continuum. So when we change our consciousness even by a small shift we may open up exciting, undreamed perspectives, and we may see that things are possible to which our former limited prospect was blind. This may be rather like a man lost in a labyrinth who suddenly finds himself lifted vertically into the air, from where he can see quite clearly the way out. Hamlet spoke truly when he said 'There are more things in heaven and earth, Horatio, than are dreamt of in your philosophy'.

In addition, the new physics seems to corroborate what mystics have always known – that observer and observed are linked, are one. When we observe something we are part of it, and we affect it, however minutely. Our picture of a Universe filled with discrete entities and objects, going their own ways, occasionally colliding but otherwise separate is another mental construct. We are all part of the web of existence, a person's life is an expression of his or her essence, rather than a chronology of events, and when we change our consciousness other changes necessarily follow. Magic is the art of directing these changes, making shifts in perception that are followed by outer events that are usually very subtle and gradual, but nonetheless real. The true goal of magic is to expand consciousness beyond our human limitations, and that is something to which we may all aspire in time.

To effect change in consciousness we use ritual, for ritual is an outward sign of inward change. By ritual and symbols we find ways to speak to our unconscious – called 'Younger Self' by Starhawk in *The Spiral Dance*. This is where herbs come in. Used in incense, oils, sachets, or just growing strong in the soil for us to touch, smell,

look at and partake of, herbs are a great help in altering consciousness. They speak directly to Younger Self, for although 'younger' in the sense of playfulness, spontaneity and creativity, Younger Self is closer to our most ancient origins, way before the Palaeolithic cave days. Herbs also have powers of their own, by virtue of their own unique essence. (In addition, the substances in some plants are hallucinogenic, able to alter the chemistry of the brain directly. These plants were ingredients in the 'flying ointments' used by the witches of yesteryear, and of course some people still use these substances today. However, we are concerned with more subtle uses, where the herbs gently help to effect change at a spiritual level, for this is much safer.)

The collective unconscious

The psychologist C. G. Jung's concept of the collective unconscious is well known. It is as if we are stratified creatures. Our conscious minds peep out like islands above the waves. Below them we have the personal unconscious, composed of our own experiences. Going deeper we come to levels of the unconscious shared by family, then lower still ethnic background, and below this our unconscious merges in a collective that we share with all humankind. But it doesn't stop there. Lower and lower down we encounter the levels of our evolution, back through mammals, reptiles and plants. The primitive, emotional part of the brain responds to scent most strongly. We have all had the sensation of suddenly being transported by a scent – back to a sunny kitchen in childhood by the smell of new-baked bread, or to the arms of an old lover by the scent of musk or jasmine. More than this, herbs remind us silently, blindly, primordially of our vegetable origins in the bowels of the Earth. They are powerful things. They speak directly to Younger Self and they can help unlock the wordless power within that is our birthright. They remind us of the days before consciousness 'separated' us and we became self-aware. In some ways magic is the blending of this ancient 'merging' with the powers of the conscious mind to formulate and direct. Herbs can help us to achieve this.

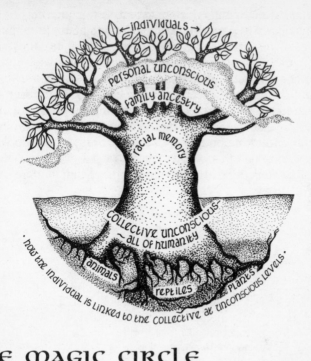

The magic circle

Magic, ritual and symbols are discussed more fully in *Witchcraft – a beginner's guide* in this series, but before we leave the subject we need to focus on the magic circle. This is a circle, or sphere, created on the spirit plane by visualisation and ritual – and such rituals usually use herbs, in incense. The circle confers protection, conserves power raised until the time for release and serves as a halfway house between this world and the Otherworld. The ritual is given in *Witchcraft – a beginner's guide*, but you can create a circle suitable for our simple purposes in this book by visualisation alone.

Just imagine a circle of blue light around you – you can 'draw' it by holding out your forefinger and imagining blue light coming from the finger tip. If you can't visualise – and some people can't, so don't be put off – then perhaps you can imagine that your circle smells of

incense, all around you, enveloping you. Or perhaps you can hear it humming, like a power cable. Maybe you are able just to engender a strong feeling of safety and containment going all around you. If all else fails, use a circular mat or something similar to aid concentration. Practise this. It is important to have your magic circle in place for anything that involves magical work of any sort, or trance work, for it will prevent you becoming depleted. Always remember to disperse your circle thoroughly when you have finished. Concentrate on this for a minute or so, as you do when forming it, although this needn't take as long as forming the circle. Eat or drink something at this point to ensure that you are fully back to Earth.

TRANCE

Much has been written about trance that is complex and portentous, but in essence it is a simple state, quite achievable by anyone, although naturally some people will more quickly and easily go into a state of deep trance, while for others the trance may be light. Much can be accomplished in light trance, however, and some people who believe they are in a light trance – during hypnotherapy, for instance – discover that they have been quite deeply hypnotised. These things are not always as dramatic as we expect, at first, but they can be extremely meaningful.

We all go through a state of trance twice a day, as we wake up and as we go to sleep. Think for a minute about the way you feel, say on a Sunday morning, when you have slept well and do not have to get up in a hurry. You are lying in bed, totally relaxed and utterly comfortable. You are drifting, but you are extremely aware. Your partner, if you have one, may be making toast in the kitchen, and the smell of it has an intense meaning for you as you lie, passively – and that meaning is much more than the thought you may be getting breakfast in bed! Comfort, pleasure, a profound sense of harmony, vivid thoughts, memories and sometimes strong insights are properties of this time.

Similarly, you may go into a trance looking at a patch of sunlight, or a candle. The world around you recedes, your consciousness alters – in fact, your brainwave pattern changes – and your internal world becomes more real than the external. You may 'forget yourself'.

Learning to achieve states of trance at will comes readily with practice. It is a process of relaxation and letting go. In this state of trance, visualisation or pathworking can be embarked upon – these are inner journeys. (In fact, the terms 'trance', 'visualisation', 'creative imagination' or 'pathworking' are often used interchangeably.) *Witchcraft – a beginner's guide* discusses guided visualisation. For our purposes in this book it will be helpful if you are able to mentally 'disconnect' such as when looking at a candle flame, and observe what goes through your mind. You can practise this if you like, by lighting a candle and staring at the flame. Try to look through it and beyond it, let your vision go blurred, let yourself feel 'far away'. Some impressions may come into your mind now and they may be interesting or significant. As you get better at this, it is best to visualise your protective circle first, so you are not open to stray energies. When finishing off breathe deeply, disperse the circle thoroughly and have something to eat or drink.

Chakras

Chakras are another subject that will be relevant to our use of herbs for healing and magic, for these are centres of spiritual energy that we can activate to help imbue our potions with the necessary power. You can still do this without using the chakras, but you will feel better and get better results if you are familiar with opening them.

Occultists believe that we have a spiritual or astral body that interpenetrates the physical, made of finer essence yet occupying the same space and shape. Some believe we have many astral bodies, each finer than the preceding and that we ascend through each of the states they represent until we reach divinity. For our purposes we need think of only one astral form, and the chakras can be seen as organs within it.

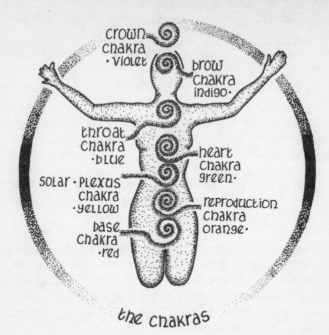

the chakras

There is more than one chakra system, for on the subtle planes maps are not rigid and we can get results in a variety of ways. The system we shall be using has seven chakras. Each of these is linked to a crucial centre in the physical body and with one of the seven colours of the visible spectrum. You can imagine each chakra as a large blossom, or wheel-shape. The first, or base chakra is coloured red and is located at the base of the spine. It is connected with roots, survival, instincts and a sense of 'where you live'. The second chakra is orange. It is found in the lower abdomen, and is the womb or testes chakra. It is connected with sexuality and sharing and also to unconscious forces within us that shape our destiny.

The third chakra is the solar plexus chakra, just behind the navel. It rules purpose, integration, willpower and independence and is coloured bright yellow, like the Sun. It is interesting that in astrology the Sun is connected to our powers of self-integration and conscious direction, as this chakra is.

The fourth, or heart chakra is located in the middle of the chest, midway between the armpits. It is coloured green and relates to compassion, caring and love – although the romantic kind of love has more to do with the second chakra. With this chakra we discover an all-embracing tenderness for our fellows and for the forces of life.

The fifth chakra is blue and located in the throat. It rules speech, communication and creativity. It is related to the Bardic arts, where words are used to conjure and empower and are a great deal more than puffs of air.

The sixth chakra is located slightly above and between the eyes, the location of the 'third eye'. Its colour is indigo and it relates to intuition, deep knowledge and appreciation of that which is beyond the everyday.

Finally, the seventh chakra, called the 'many-petalled lotus' or crown chakra is found at the top of the head, and it is coloured violet. This chakra is the most transcendent or rarified and it is associated with mysticism, union with the Divine and a true sense of Self.

Some writers regard opening the chakras as a matter for aspiring spiritual adepts, whereas others have a more pragmatic approach. I am of the latter group, although like anything else opening the chakras has different levels. Riding a bike does not automatically qualify you for the Tour de France! As you learn to open your chakras you will get better and better at it and feel more uplifted. Besides, areas of life that need healing – for instance, sexuality – can be helped by 'working on' or concentrating on the relevant chakra, unblocking it, expanding it, and purifying it.

OPENING YOUR CHAKRAS

This is a simple matter, but may take some practice. When it happens it may not be dramatic, so please don't expect suddenly to see the whole world clothed in light as your chakra awareness begins. We have space here for only a brief look at opening chakras, so I would recommend further reading on this, starting with *Chakras for Beginners* by Naomi Ozaniec, in this series.

First you will need to learn how to relax, and that is also essential for trance work. Our habitual tension, of which we are mostly not even aware, stands between us and many things – clear vision, concentration, revelation, true fulfilment and, of course, success in magical endeavours.

As you read this book become aware of your body and run through a quick checklist for tension. The neck is a favourite location – is it knotted, rigid, head inclined slightly forwards? What about your shoulders? Are they hunched in perpetual self-protection against – what? Are your teeth gritted? Fists clenched? Is there a centre of tension in your stomach? Or are your leg muscles clenched, your toes pointed? Areas of habitual tension are where you may need to concentrate especially as you learn to relax.

You should spend about ten minutes **each day** on relaxation practice – longer sessions at more widely spaced intervals won't do. Lie on your bed and tense each muscle in turn starting at your toes and working upwards. Tense each to the point of extremity – but watch out for cramp! Then relax. When you have gone all the way up your body – and there are many, many muscles around the head and face – mentally check again to make sure no tension has crept back.

The method I prefer is to imagine that you are a candle with a flame burning at the top of your head. All the soft, warm wax is running down over your body, taking away all tension with it. You could similarly use the imagery of being under a warm shower, but the candle method has the advantage that the symbolism is reminiscent of the crown chakra, glowing.

When you are satisfied that you can relax at will – and if you are a complete beginner this will probably take several weeks of practice, for this is a stage that should not be rushed – you can try to open your chakras. Begin with the base chakra. Concentrate on its locality and colour, and you may like to repeat inwardly the characteristics you associate with it. Do not try to force anything, for again this may take weeks. You will probably feel a sense of excitement or mild, pleasurable electric shock as the chakra begins to open. You

may twitch and the colour of the chakra may seem to flood your being. Keep an open mind, for everyone's experience is different. When you have opened the first chakra do not rush onwards. Linger, immersing yourself in the pleasurable sensation. Be conscious of drawing power up, from the earth, into your base chakra.

Then slowly draw the power up to the second chakra. Feel it opening, glowing, gaining in strength until it is fully functioning. Concentrate on the colour in question. Then go on to the next chakra, and the next, until all your chakras are open and you feel sublime and shining.

You are now well prepared for any magical or trance work you have planned. Your chakras will stay open, you do not have to concentrate on keeping them that way, although it is advisable to practise a few times before going on to any workings. However, there are several important points to be born in mind.

First, always make sure that you won't be disturbed while opening your chakras. If someone comes charging into the room or a child starts screaming you may well feel sick and disorientated.

Second, always close your chakras thoroughly after opening. Imagine them closing like flower petals in the rain, like sleepy eyes, like doors – or whatever appeals. Have a bite to eat and something to drink and take a few deep breaths. Please do this even if you don't feel you've opened your chakras. In our sceptical, materialistic world we often talk ourselves out of experiences. The psychologist Maslow observed that people may have peak experiences without recognising them as such! So ensure that your chakras are not accidentally open by being aware of this.

Third, do not open your chakras when you are with anyone who makes you uneasy, especially someone who you feel sucks your energy in whatever way, or who may wish to attack you in however subtle a manner. This book is not about group working, but it is something to be born in mind.

Fourth, having opened the chakras, daily practice is not needed. The purpose of relaxing daily is to get the relaxation routine and message firmly embedded in your subconscious. Once this is

accomplished, however, daily trance and chakra work may make you unfit for ordinary life, unless you are in retreat. This is an individual matter, but be careful not to become spaced-out and over-subjective.

Opening your chakras is worthwhile in itself, because it increases your level of awareness of spiritual, subtle matters. Later on we shall be looking at how to use chakra energies in healing and magic – once the chakras are open this is fairly simple.

Ethics

These are an individual matter and there are no dogmas. However, the one rule that is disregarded at peril is 'Harm none'. Whatever magical work you engage in, ensure that your motives are pure. Pure in this sense doesn't mean without desire or self-interest, for these are part of being human. But it does mean being careful not to harm or coerce anyone else. Tradition says that anything harmful will return to sender threefold, and as you become magically aware you will know that you and your actions are one strand of being. If you are malevolent you will certainly harm yourself in some way. A positive approach is always best.

Correspondences

Books on magic usually speak of correspondences. These are lists – sometimes very long lists – of substances, plants, days, colours, planets, symbols that harmonise. They are used in the 'like attracts like' principle. So the Moon is associated with healing, with silver, with Monday, with pearl and moonstone, and of course with many herbs, such as lemon balm, calamus, camphor, willow. So for a healing spell we might employ a selection of these ingredients, and perform our spell on Monday, preferably by the light of the Full Moon.

The most well-known system of correspondences comes from the ancient body of mystical knowledge called the Qabalah. However

there are other systems. For instance the Celtic (or pre-Celtic) Ogham alphabet (pronounced O'am) associates each letter with a tree and many other objects and creatures such as birds, minerals, ideas. There is some dispute about how ancient this system of correspondences may be, but it is nonetheless valid. For correspondences are not, as it may seem, the dry and complex way of the mind to reduce the Universe to formulae.

It may be useful to imagine a spider's web, pearled by dew and glistening in the sunrise. Each dewdrop becomes a rainbow. The web is complex, and fascinatingly beautiful. All parts are interconnected and if you twitch one strand the entire web quivers, albeit very gently. Now if this can be extended to the picture of a three-dimensional web, of transcendent beauty and infinite extent we are coming close to a magical perception of the Universe. Everything, from ourselves to the furthest stars is connected in this web. All we do affects everything else, in however small a way. All is associated and interconnected.

Systems of correspondences enable us to move about this framework to some extent. They show us things that are threaded on the same strand. The fact that different systems give different associations does not matter, for this is not a doctrine, or a dogma, but a way of working, and one method may serve as well as another for getting to our goal. However, correspondences are more than this. They are a wonderful aid to memory, for when such links are built up it is possible to recall a great deal by association. In addition, it is wonderfully stimulating to the imagination and brings all of existence to life and fills it with poetry. Paintings, poems, ideas all may rise from these correlations.

Needless to say, herbs fit into systems of correspondence and are very important. The system I shall be using in this book is the astrological one, which is also linked to the Qabalah, although we shall not be concerning ourselves with that. Most people know something of astrology and so it is the most simple and evocative. Of course, nothing is rigid, and you are free to make up your own mind, for your experience of a herb may incline you to a different association.

Let us take an example of sunflower and chamomile. These are both ruled by the Sun, and yet they are very different. The sunflower, looking so bright, friendly, garish gives the impression of devil-may-care, 'I'm-up-for-anything' confidence. And yet it is an annual plant, not easy to grow and surprisingly prone, if conditions are in any way inclement, to drooping and early death. So we may think in terms of the Sun's 'death' each year as winter comes, and how ephemeral life can be. The sunflower has links with the Leonine personality – the sign Leo is ruled by the Sun, which means that the Sun has an affinity with Leo. Leo people may seem confident and lordly but in reality they are sensitive and may be quite crushed by lack of attention. Chamomile on the other hand is much tougher. Unassuming and fragrant it will grow into a lawn and has many health-giving properties. So chamomile speaks more of the envigorating, energising and enduring aspects of the Sun. If we were wishing to combine Sun and Moon energies for a ritual we might pick chamomile to represent the Sun (depending, of course, on what our purpose might be) feeling that it might harmonise better with a Moon herb – perhaps lemon balm – rather better than any part of the sunflower. Of course, this is a personal thing. The above is merely offered as an example.

The planetary correspondences we shall be using are listed below. It will help you if you can get the basic idea lodged in your memory, so that when you think 'Mercury' you automatically think 'light, airy, mental, communicative' and so your ideas will spin out from there.

SUN

Obviously the largest body in our solar system, giving heat and light to all.

Keywords

Health, protection, success, enlightenment, power, energy, integration, purpose, consciousness, potential, growth.

OTHER ASSOCIATIONS

Gods Apollo, Lugh, Ra. Orange or gold. Amber, diamond, tiger's eye, sunstone. Rules Leo (sometimes associated with Aries and Sagittarius). Sunday.

MOON

Just as large in the sky as the Sun, when full. The Moon shines at night, time of the secret, the magical, the enchanting, the subtle. Rules the tides, the ebb and flow of instinctual and bodily rhythms.

KEYWORDS

Fertility, home, instinct, the subconscious, family, healing, gardening, meaningful dreams, rhythm, caring, spirituality.

OTHER ASSOCIATIONS

Goddesses Brigid, Dana, Levanah, Diana, the Great Mother. White or silver. Aquamarine, chalcedony, quartz, moonstone. Rules Cancer (sometimes links with Taurus and Pisces, dark and waning Moon Scorpio). Monday.

MERCURY

Smallest, swiftest planet, nearest the Sun, named after the Roman god with wings on his heels.

KEYWORDS

Airy, quick, light, intellectual, communicative, eloquence, study, travel.

OTHER ASSOCIATIONS

Gods Mercury, Hermes, Woden/Odin, Thoth. Yellow. Agate, aventurine, mottled jasper. Rules Gemini and Virgo. Links also with Aquarius. Wednesday.

VENUS

Nearest planet to us, brightest and most beautiful, appearing in the rosy skies of dawn or dusk, when lovemaking often takes place. Named after goddess of love and beauty.

Keywords

Beauty, harmony, reconciliation, youth, happiness, pleasure, compassion, relating.

Other associations

Goddesses Venus, Aphrodite, Freya. Green – possibly soft blue and rose. Emerald, lapis-lazuli, turquoise (sometimes rose quartz). Rules the signs Libra and Taurus (sometimes associated with Pisces, and occasionally Cancer). Friday.

MARS

The red planet, named after the god of war.

Keywords

Anger, aggression, assertion, action, courage, strength, healing (after surgery) sexuality, menstruation, defence.

Other associations

Gods Mars, Ares, Thor. Red. Bloodstone, flint, garnet, ruby. Rules Aries and is the old ruler of Scorpio. Thursday.

JUPITER

Largest planet in the solar system, we now realise how Jupiter has literally 'protected' us, by its strong gravitational field, from frequent devastation by collision with large meteorites.

Keywords

Expansion, optimism, confidence, prosperity, legal settlements, religion, spirituality, meditation, psychism, preservation.

Other associations

Gods Jupiter, Zeus, Tiw/Tir. Purple, royal blue. Amethyst, lepidolite. Rules the signs Sagittarius and is the old ruler of Pisces (occasionally may have association with Cancer). Tuesday.

SATURN

Planet surrounded by rings, used to be thought the boundary of the solar system.

Keywords

Restriction, contraction, concentration, discipline, binding, grounding, centering, purifying (sometimes luck, fertility, nurturing and sexuality).

Other associations

Gods Saturn, Chronos, The Horned God Herne/Cernunnos. Brown, black, grey, dark green or blue. Jet, onyx, obsidian. Rules the signs Capricorn and is the old ruler of Aquarius (occasionally may have links with Libra). Saturday.

***

You may notice that the three outer planets Uranus, Neptune and Pluto are not included as most correspondences were made before these were discovered – although thinking about these can expand awareness.

Later on we shall be talking about herbs being 'ruled by' or 'under' one of the listed planets, which will give rise to a host of associations of which the above can be only a small example. Occasionally there is more than one rulership, or you may feel that a herb is linked to a planet other than that which I specify. This is important for you and you should take it into consideration when

using the herbs. We shall be looking at how to strengthen your ability to make your own associations later on.

practice

Find a suitable notebook in which to begin recording correspondences. Devote a page to each of the planets and write down everything you can think of that you associate with it. What do you know about the mythology of the gods linked to the planets? With what sorts of things do you think the planetary energies might help? What might they make worse? For instance, Venusian energies are obviously good for love, patching quarrels, being creative, but they won't be very helpful to someone who needs to protect him or herself against someone who is being invasive and attacking. Later we shall consider which herbs are associated with which planetary energies.

Teach Yourself Astrology by Jeff Mayo (Hodder & Stoughton, 1996) describes each of the planets more fully. Books on mythology for older children are often clear and interesting – Roger Lancelyn Green is a good author. You may find such books helpful to get you in tune with planetary energies, if this idea is new to you. Do not be afraid to scribble down anything you like. You may wish to alter your associations later on, and that is fine.

It is a good idea at this stage to have another small notebook – perhaps an address book, for that will have pages alphabetically marked – for making notes about herbs. Keep your associations/ correspondences notes, alphabetical herbal index and any recipes/combinations of your own, together in a file.

If you wish to practise relaxation and opening your chakras you may like to begin your daily routine now and do some extra study on chakras.

CHAPTER 2

HERBS

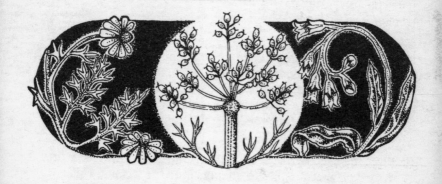

Good Mother Honey, Good Mother Honey,
So plays the hymn of the fruit and the seed
Good Mother Honey, Good Mother Honey,
So turns the dance of the herb and the hive ....

Carolyn Hillyer, 'Good Mother Honey' from the album
Grandmother Turtle, a Circle of Thirteen, Seventh Wave
Music, 1995

*H*erbs have served humankind for many thousands of years, since the time when the ancient hunter-gatherers evolved into a society that cultivated plants as foodstuff. The secrets of the soil, the miracle of growing shoots, the provision of food – all this was the province of women. Growing crops was a sacred act of participation in the Goddess, for all life was contained within Her.

Herbs are a basic product of Nature – most of them have been around in their present form for many thousands of years. They are not refined hybrids, but humble, tough and useful offerings of the Earth herself. Contact with herbs, growing them and handling them helps us to get a sense of our own roots, in the same mother soil. We have a nostalgia for 'the natural' and herbs fulfil this need. Besides this they have many practical and nutritional qualities that we appreciate more as the taste for organic crops increases. It is not far-fetched to say that increasing incidence of food poisoning may be connected to less frequent use of herbs, for they have natural antiseptic properties.

Use of herbs is documented from as long ago as 3000 BCE (Before Common Era – a term preferred by pagans) in ancient Babylon. Herbs were greatly respected in ancient China, India and Egypt. The Greeks, too, valued herbs, and made attempts to remove superstition from their use. (Superstition, by the way, is different from magic. Believing that 'the bogey-man won't get you if you avoid the cracks in the pavement' is quite different from conscious, directed, magical intent.)

The Romans used herbs extensively, planting them wherever they went and carrying supplies to administer to the legions. This is documented by the surgeon Dioscorides, author of the oldest surviving herbal, from 512 CE. Many of the herbs familiar in the United Kingdom were brought by the Roman legions, and the majority of herbs flourish in all temperate latitudes.

We are all familiar with the witch-hunt hysteria of the Middle Ages, and it was during those times that much herbal wisdom went 'underground'. Medicine, such as it was, became the property of the well-off and educated. The healing arts of the old priestesses were lost, or distorted, and anyone who practised them risked the charge of sorcery. Nonetheless, much herbal lore did live on, by word of mouth, handed down through the generations, and we are trying to rediscover this today, piecing together history and re-honing our powers of intuition, as once more we also find the Goddess.

Speaking of 'intuition', this is a faculty often associated with darkened rooms, arcane symbols and occult artefacts, and it is true that these give room to manoeuvre to the subconscious mind. However, it is contact with Nature that really gives muscle to the intuition. Go for walks in the rain, or in the winter's dusk, watch the cloud pictures, feel the Earth-power pulsing through the soles of your feet. Close your eyes. What do you see, now, with your mind's eye? How do you feel? Plant herbs, stroke their leaves, run the soil through your fingers. Exercise your intuition in daily life. Where do you think you may find that special present that you have been looking for? Which corner of the garden will best suit your new plant? Which of the job adverts you are looking through 'feels right'? Instincts often help us with such questions. And so through contact with the natural world and through trust, intuition grows.

GROWING HERBS

If you wish to use herbs for magic and ritual, you really need to grow your own. I don't believe it is necessary to grow every herb you are likely to use. Nor do you have to use a herb from your garden when dried herbs are readily available and your plant is only small. For instance, I grow lemon balm, but I buy the lemon balm I use in incense because it is cheap and easy. But growing a plant connects you to the group soul of that species, and you are listening to the plant's 'story'.

You don't have to be an expert gardener to grow herbs, for they are mostly resilient and enthusiastic. Take a basic note of whether they prefer sun or shade, plant them in the ground and leave them to get on with it. My father-in-law, himself the son of a gardener, taught me the 'two choice' rule of gardening – 'It either will or it won't'. Most things want to live, and so they 'will'. Fussing over plants can be the worst thing you can do. With this rule in mind I forge ahead, planting anything and everything, often quite roughly. When you lead a busy life there is not always time to be gentle, but I must admit I usually whisper a few words of encouragement and welcome

to new plants. In so doing I rediscover the green fingers I had as a child, transplanting plants several times, occasionally with half their roots, yet still they flourish!

Unless you live in tropical or arctic conditions there are sure to be herbs you can grow in your part of the world. In the United Kingdom at any rate a selection of herbs is readily available in most good garden centres. If you do not have a garden, don't be discouraged. Many herbs can be grown in window boxes, and it is still worthwhile to grow just a few. Always keep things simple and manageable for yourself. Buy herbs you like or feel attracted to, even if it's just because of the name. If you have a full-time job don't overstretch yourself by getting loads of plants, for although herbs need little care, they do sometimes get eaten by slugs, and one thing they will need, if the summer is long and dry, is daily watering. So start small, perhaps with names that are familiar to you, and enjoy the fascination of growing things.

PLANTING AND HARVESTING

Herb seeds are best planted during the Moon's first quarter – this means in the first seven days after New Moon. Lunar phases are shown in many calendars and diaries. It is best to wait for a day or so after New Moon, for the cycle to establish itself, for when the Moon is very new it is in the same sign of the zodiac as the Sun, and that can be overwhelming and unpredictable. However, if there has been a drought, wait for Full Moon.

Herbs can be gathered during a waxing Moon, but if they are for use in herbal remedies, or if you intend to dry them it is best to wait until the Moon's third quarter – that is, the seven days following Full Moon. In the final seven days approaching New Moon, little gardening activity is recommended, apart from pruning and spraying.

Some spells, namely 'wanions' or banishing spells are best performed with a waning Moon. The instructions for certain spells specify that the plant be cut when the Moon is waning. Opinions vary as to how important this sort of timing may be. I think the

phase of the Moon is important, but not essential. If you have a sick child you won't want to wait a week to harvest healing herbs. Similarly, a spell concerning a specific event, like an interview or an exam might not wait until the correct phase. In respect of planting, I have found plants put in when the Moon is waning usually do fine, although they may take longer to get going.

Herbs are traditionally cut with a white-handled knife – at least, this is believed to be tradition and it has been adopted by some present-day practitioners. It doesn't really matter what you cut the herbs with, and scissors are usually most practical. However, it is probably better to have a special pair of scissors or Swiss army knife for cutting herbs for use in ritual, as then by association, you get in the right frame of mind as soon as you pick up your implement. In former times, however, poor people wouldn't have been able to afford to have several knives.

As an example, for the 'Psychism and Dreams Bath' given in Chapter 5 I feel it is preferable to harvest the bay, thyme and rose petals, if you are growing them yourself, by the light of the Full Moon and prepare an infusion for use the same night. Such things are important, but it is their effect on you that matters most, so look into your heart and go with what feels right, not a rule book.

Empowering Herbs

This can start when you harvest your herbs. It really means holding the purpose for which the herbs are to be used in your mind, as you maintain a relaxed, somewhat dreamy state. When the herbs are gathered, assuming they are all to be used for the same purpose, place your hands over them and visualise your vital energy entering them, all the while imagining the magical intent. You might like to repeat a few words such as 'Rosemary, rosemary, strengthen mind'. This is best done by candle or moonlight, within the magic circle, with open chakras. Remember to close down thoroughly after you have empowered your herbs.

Drying herbs

Drying herbs should begin as soon as the plant is harvested, but should not be too swift. Dry herbs separately. Clean leaves and dry them at about 30 °C for the first day, thereafter at about 25 °C. A large airing cupboard is ideal for drying. Some herbs can be hung in bundles by their stems and that looks attractive. Flowers can be treated similarly. Roots, being tougher, can be dried in an oven at about 55 °C. Bark should be dried out in a dry, warm place. Store all produce in airtight jars, clearly labelled with name and date. If condensation forms the produce wasn't really dry so take the herbs out and finish the process. Like many other activities, drying herbs needs skill and practice but this comes with experience.

Characteristics and herbal lore

We can now look at a selection of familiar herbs, their characteristics and lore in a little more detail.

BASIL

Ocimum basilicum. Basil is a tender annual that grows to about 45 cm in height. It likes warmth, but needs to be protected from extremes, such as frost and gales and unrelenting exposure to scorching midday sun. It has a 'round' spicy flavour and is often used in cooking.

Basil is ruled by Mars and associated with the sign Scorpio. This herb is native to India where it was sacred to the god Vishnu. Oaths were sworn upon it in court. Bush basil grows in South America and is sacred to the Haitian love goddess, Erzulie.

Magically basil is used for love, wealth, exorcism and protection. Its heart-warming properties soothe strife between lovers and it can be used as a simple perfume, created by rubbing leaves against the skin until their fragrance is released. Carrying basil in your pocket attracts wealth, and it is regularly added to incense in love spells and purification rituals. It can be placed or strewn anywhere that you wish to have cleansed.

This is a lovely, fragrant plant, good for the digestion.

BAY

Laurus nobilis. Bay is an evergreen tree. However, if the weather is very cold the leaves may wither, especially in young plants. The bay tree will grow to 7 m in height and can be made into a hedge, cut into all sorts of intriguing shapes. It likes full sun (but can survive with less) and the leaves can be picked at any time.

Bay is ruled by the Sun and was sacred to the Greek sun-god, Apollo. His temple at Delphi was the site of the well-known Delphic oracle (the site having been taken over from the earlier mother-goddess). The roof of the temple was made from bay leaves, for protection of the Oracle, who would no doubt have been vulnerable when she was in a state of trance. We can still use bay in incense as a protection during meditation or ritual. Bay leaves were chewed by the priestess and, because they have a slightly narcotic quality, they may have helped to bring about the prophetic trance – bay is of the laurel family, and chewing one's laurels makes an interesting change from resting on them!

Magically bay is used for strength, prophecy, healing, protection and purification. Bay guards against lightning, and it is said that no bay tree has ever been struck. Keep bay leaves with you to give you prowess during sporting events and to ward off negativity. Place leaves beneath your pillow for meaningful dreams or pin five leaves to your pillow to dream of the person you will marry.

Bay is well known as an aromatic addition to juicy casseroles.

CHAMOMILE

Chamaemelum nobile (Anthemis nobilis). Chamomile is a hardy, evergreen perennial that likes full sun or some shade. In full sun it may reach 20 cm, in shade 30 cm. Chamomile can be grown as a lawn, and is a great friend to other plants, seeming to help along anything placed near it.

Chamomile is ruled by the Sun. It is also called Ground Apple, because the leaves, when rubbed, have an apple-like scent. Sir Francis Drake, of Armada fame, is said to have played his nonchalant game of bowls on a chamomile lawn. Witches were believed to have helped to defeat the Armada through the storms they whistled up, and the great Sir Francis himself is believed to have been a witch. I can't help wondering if the game of bowls was an impromptu spell, using the protective essence of chamomile as a background to Sir Francis's concentration. Although ruled by the Sun, chamomile is associated with the element Water – did the lawn represent the ocean, and the bowls certain ships? I believe this is more than idle speculation, because if Drake really was a witch it would have been natural to use his 'game' in that way, and of course he would have appeared calm and 'centred' as he played.

Chamomile was the sedative given in Beatrix Potter's story to greedy Peter Rabbit after his adventure in Mr McGregor's garden. It is used in many remedies both internally and externally (as *Chamomilla recutita*). It is relaxing, good for morning sickness, nausea, digestive troubles and urinary infections. Magically it is used for sleep, love, purification and money – washing your hands in an infusion is said to attract luck when gambling.

COMFREY

Symphytum officinale. A hardy herbaceous perennial, comfrey can attain a height of just over a metre. Comfrey likes full sun, and its roots go very deep – 3 m in fact – so once established in place it will be hard to uproot!

Comfrey is ruled by Saturn. It isn't very attractive, unless the little mauve flowers are out, but it has a comforting stability about it. Garden herbs ruled by Saturn are not very plentiful, and Saturn has the rulership of some well-known 'nasties' like hemlock, which may be fascinating but best avoided if you have curious children. So I've included comfrey partly for its rulership, and also just because I like it. Herbs are like that – one somehow can't help developing a relationship with them.

Comfrey is used magically for money and safe travel. Put some comfrey leaves in your briefcase or among your clean underwear in your suitcase. Comfrey leaves are rich in vitamins A, C and B12 and have a great deal of protein in their structure – which is what you'd expect of solid Saturn. Comfrey leaves are good placed on bruises, cuts, burns and sprains. There are some doubts about the long-term effects of taking comfrey internally, but these have still to be proved. It is good for treating bronchitis and gastric upsets.

COWSLIP AND PRIMROSE

Primula veris and *Primula vulgaris*. Not always thought of as herbs, these brave, cheerful little plants deserve to be included for being heralds of the English spring. They are hardy herbaceous perennials. Cowslips grow to about 23 cm, primroses to 15 cm. They nestle, spots of gold, under the hedges. When I was a child they seemed like a gift of the fairies and I thought they might disappear if I took my eyes off them. Truly they seemed real earth magic.

Now, of course, it is illegal to take the flowers from the wild, but you can buy them in pots, use them to celebrate the Spring Equinox, and plant them out in the garden to multiply. They are both ruled by Venus, and both the primrose and the little cowslip bell have five petals. Five is the number of the Goddess, reminiscent of the five-point star or pentagram that is often used in magic. Cowslip, held in the hand, can be used to find treasure. Magically it is also good for healing and to restore youth. Primroses are used for protection and love. If you have plenty of primroses growing in your garden you might like to press some as a token for someone's birthday. Flowers

are an ancient token of emotion – indeed there are 'flower alphabets', emphasising the phrase 'Say it with flowers'. Cowslips and primroses speak of hope, promise and affection.

An infusion of primrose can be a remedy for coughs.

FENNEL

Foeniculum vulgare. Fennel is a hardy, herbaceous perennial that grows to just over 2 m and likes to be planted in full sun. It is an attractive plant, with its delicate, web-like leaves, and the bronze-leaved variety is the prettiest.

This plant is ruled by Mercury, but is also associated with the Titan Prometheus, who brought the gift of fire to humankind, with such dire results for himself, for Zeus, king of the Gods, decreed that Prometheus should be chained to a mountainside and his liver eaten by an eagle. Each night the liver grew back; each day the eagle feasted on it. Eventually Prometheus was rescued by Hercules, and fennel may be connected with him because it is used for purification, protection and healing, and has, therefore, been prized for many centuries. The plant is totally edible, from seed to root. It was valued by the Romans for its health-giving powers, and it was sacred to the Anglo-Saxons because of its power to ward off evil.

Fennel can be hung at windows and doors to keep away anything harmful or negative, placed in keyholes to keep out ghosts and it can be added to herbal sachets for purification. It is known for its mild, aniseed flavour as herbal tea. It is good for combating flatulence and constipation. It may reduce the ill effects of alcohol, and is said to regulate body weight, if taken regularly.

FEVERFEW

Tanacetum parthenium (Chrysanthemum parthenium). Feverfew is a hardy perennial, growing to about 60 cm in height. It prefers a sunny position, but seems to grow almost anywhere and the daisy-like flowers stay open for ages.

Feverfew is ruled by Venus, and its main magical use is for protection. Take a few leaves with you in your pocket when you are going anywhere that you feel may hold danger – of infection, accident or even emotional hurt.

This plant is also called Bachelor's Buttons. Marion Green (in *The Magical Lore of Herbs*) says that gentlemen wishing to attract their lady-love should carry this in their pockets – even growing the plant in their pockets, according to old stories!

Feverfew's best-known healing quality is in the relief of headaches and migraine, and recent scientific research supports this. Three to five fresh leaves eaten daily in a sandwich may well reduce the frequency and intensity of this distressing malady.

LAVENDER

Lavendula angustifolia, L. officinalis or *L. spica*. Lavender is a hardy, evergreen shrub that grows to about 1 m in height. It is well known for being extremely fragrant, and has small flowers of blue, purple, white or pale pink. It thrives in a sunny, open position, it is very easy to grow and can be used to form a sweet-smelling hedge.

Lavender is ruled by Mercury, the planet of communication and swift thought. Hermes/Mercury was a versatile god who acted as escort to the dead, because he was one of the few among gods and mortals who could enter the Underworld and return. Psychologically, an implication may be that the gap between the 'Underworld' or unconscious and the daylight, conscious realm can be bridged by a flexible approach – in other words by Mercury and all associated with him. So we can link the 'mercurial' function in the human mind to clarity and sanity. This leads to balance and relaxation – so no wonder that this mercurial herb can soothe headaches, anxiety and sleeplessness.

We may associate lavender with stately Victoriana, and I have heard it called 'an old lady's scent' rather unfairly, for it is envigorating and youthful in character. The Greeks and Romans loved to sprinkle it in their bath water, and the name is derived from the Latin *lavare*

meaning 'to wash'. Its fragrance is enduring, and because of this it was strewn on floors in Medieval and Tudor times. Lavender repels insects and was useful to mask odours in times when people lived in close proximity to much that was unclean.

Magical uses of lavender are many. They include purification, happiness, love, protection, sleep, peace and longevity. It is generally helpful for any process that requires clear thought, divination, study, concentration and visualisation. So if you have an exam or important interview coming up, place just a little lavender oil on your pillow the night before and sprinkle a few drops on a handkerchief to take with you. Sniff it when you need to collect your thoughts and clear your head, to give you the extra bit of help you need.

LEMON BALM

Melissa officinalis. A hardy, herbaceous perennial, lemon balm grows to a height of about 1 m. It prefers a sunny position but is most comfortable if not exposed to the heat of the midday sun. The leaves can be picked at any time, but are most flavoursome when the plant is coming into flower.

Lemon balm is ruled by the Moon. Diana is one of many Moon Goddesses, and this plant was sacred to her temple. Some amazing healing properties have been attributed to this plant. Pliny said that if it was placed on a sword that had caused a wound, the flow of blood would cease immediately. Parecelsus believed it could revive a person completely. Two very long-lived men are believed to owe their longevity to regularly taking lemon balm tea – Llewellyn, Prince of Glamorgan in the thirteenth century, who lived to be 108, and John Hussey, from Sydenham in England, who lived to 116.

Magical uses of the herb include love, healing and general success. I connect it also with fertility. Lemon balm can be infused in wine as a love potion, or you may carry it with you to help you find love. It is also said to attract bees. If you keep them, rub this herb on the hive to retain them and entice new bees.

mallow

Althaea officinalis. I grow mallow because of the baby softness of the underside of the leaves. Also called marsh mallow, it is a hardy herbaceous perennial that can reach a height of 2 m. It prefers full sun.

Marsh mallow is the original source of the synthetic sweet that now has the same name. The root, when powdered, contains a mucilage that goes thick in water. Heated with sugar it forms a sweet, but the packeted marshmallow that we buy contains none of the original herb. Mallow was eaten by the Romans and Egyptians.

Mallow is used magically for exorcism, protection and love. It is ruled by the Moon. Mallow is another herb that can be carried to attract love, and if your lover has left you, a vase of mallow placed outside door or window will, it is said, draw him or her back to you.

Medicinally mallow is good for treating inflammations, both internal and external. Its considerable mucilage content helps the body's defence system to work, as it is soothing. It is recommended for coughs, laryngitis, boils, bronchitis and urinary infections.

mint

Mentha species. Mints are hardy herbaceous perennials. Some types grow as high as 1 m, while other varieties provide good ground cover. Partial shade or full sun is suitable for this herb.

Mint is one of the best-loved culinary herbs, well known as the main ingredient of the mint sauce that goes with roast lamb, and good for putting in the water when cooking new potatoes. It is ruled by Venus, or Mercury, depending on whom you consult and I have seen peppermint (*Mentha piperita*) given with Mars as ruler also.

Mint is also associated with the Underworld deities Pluto and Hecate, and one story says that Minthe was a nymph with whom Pluto fell in love. He changed her into a mint plant to save her from the wrath of Persephone, his wife – to be changed into vegetation was the fate of many nymphs pursued by gods, but in this way they received a life that was ever-renewing.

Magically mint is used in spells for travel, exorcism, protection, money, lust and healing. Put a few leaves next to your money, to make it grow. Placing mint on the altar is supposed to draw good influences towards your rituals and magic. In the summer I often place a sprig of mint on the household shrine, next to our goddess figure, as an offering – for it grows plentifully and smells refreshing. Peppermint is used for sleep, love, healing, psychism and purification, and if placed beneath the pillow you may see the future in your dreams – if that is what you want.

Peppermint is well known for its power to relieve indigestion and calm the stomach. It is also good for combating fever and morning sickness, but the essential oil should be avoided in pregnancy.

PARSLEY

Petroselinum crispum. Parsley is a hardy biennial. It is happy in full sun or light shade and grows to about 35 cm in height. The purity of the green in its leaves is almost luminous. It is said the plant, grown next to roses, makes them healthy and enhances their fragrance.

This is another well-known herb used in cooking, notable in parsley sauce, served with fish. It is ruled by Mercury and used magically to protect, purify and provoke lust. It is also associated with Queen of the Underworld, Persephone, and it has quite a few daunting associations with death and evil. It should not be cut if you are in love, lest you cut your love (I don't know if that means you'll harm the emotional flow or literally cause the one you love to be cut). The Greeks left parsley on graves, and it has some association with brews made for black magic. It is said it will grow only for the head of the household, so that could be revealing! The Romans wore parsley garlands on the head to delay drunkenness.

Chew raw parsley for fresh breath – it is said to take away the odour of garlic. The infusion can be a tonic to the digestion. Parsley is rich in vitamin C, also in vitamins A and B. In pregnancy its consumption should be moderate. Despite its bad reputation, parsley was worn by the Romans on their togas, for protection.

ROSE

Rosa species. These are hardy shrubs and many gardeners make an absorbing hobby out of rearing roses and waging an eternal battle against the many pests that seem to love this most fragrant of plants. Personally, I prefer the wild rose, or dog rose, *Rosa canina* which rambles everywhere and provides the rose 'hips' that are rich in vitamin C. Roses are said to attract fairies, or nature spirits, where they are grown.

The planetary ruler of the rose is Venus, but it is associated with many deities, including Isis and Demeter. Its magical powers are many and include love – of course – healing, divination concerning love, psychism, luck and protection. Roses can be worn during a love ritual, to give extra power to the work. In flower-language red roses are well known for saying 'I love you'. This is the passionate sort of love. White roses, on the other hand mean discretion and silence. One legend says that all roses were once white, but Cupid shot a dart at a bush and made it bleed.

This beautiful plant also has a connection with war. In England the Wars of the Roses, named after the rose symbols of the rival houses of York and Lancaster, were waged for centuries, until both houses were united in the Tudor rose, when Henry Tudor (Henry VII) married Elizabeth of York.

The essential oil of rose is very expensive, but an infusion can be made from the petals and added to bathwater as a love spell. The rose calms anger and discordant emotions in true Venusian style. Rosewater is a good antidote for headaches. This is another plant that can be carried for protection, and the petals can be dried and used in incense.

ROSEMARY

Rosemarinus officinalis. Rosemary is a hardy, evergreen perennial that can reach a height of 2 m. It has small flowers of white, pink or blue. The flowers are said to have been white originally, but they turned

blue when the Virgin Mary laid her mantle over them. It prefers a sunny site and needs to be protected from biting winds.

This herb is ruled by the Sun. Magically it promotes sleep, enduring youth, protection, love, lust, mental awareness and purification. It is an ancient ingredient of incense, and can be burnt for purification or to receive insight. The smoke can be inhaled to promote vision and 'the sight'. It can be used as a substitute for frankincense – although personally I don't think there is **any** substitute for the rich beauty of frankincense, in some ways, magically rosemary will do fine. Carry rosemary for health, and place it underneath your bed for safe and peaceful sleep. Rosemary is also added to wedding chaplets and bouquets, meaning fidelity.

Medicinally, rosemary is good for convalescence, and for relieving depression and exhaustion following severe stress. It is also good for the circulation – rather as one might expect from this 'sunny' herb.

SAGE

Salvia officinalis. Sage is a hardy, evergreen shrub that may grow to a height of 75 cm. It prefers full sun. Most sage varieties have mauve flowers, but less frequently white and pink flowers are seen. Clary sage is a biennial variety of the plant. It is considered unlucky for sage to have a herb bed to itself, so ensure it has some companions.

Hearty sage has the planetary rulership of Jupiter. Claims about its wonderful properties date from ancient times. An old proverb said 'How can a man die who has sage in his garden?' 'Salvia' is derived from the Latin *salvere*, which means 'to save, cure or to thrive'. Magical uses of sage include money, protection, longevity, wisdom and the granting of wishes. Carry sage if you wish to be wise. Eat a little daily – especially in May – if you want a long life. Sage can also be burnt as incense.

Like many household herbs, sage was said to grow well when the woman was in charge. It is possible that this relates to the Bronze Age and before, when women probably did have control of growing crops, temple rites and much more. By all accounts these times were

much more peaceful than our own. However, matriarchy does not mean having a woman in charge in the same way as a man may rule under patriarchy. It means a different, 'feminine' set of values, where communication, connectedness, home, harmony and caring are set above domination and conquest. So there is no reason why a luxuriant herb garden should mean a bossy female rules the roost! More subtly, it may mean gentler values are paramount.

Sage has antiseptic properties. It is traditionally served with pork and poultry, and it is possible that such combinations help the body to cope with the toxicity that may be present in the meat. Medicinally an infusion of sage leaves is good for sore throats and mouth ulcers. Sage should be avoided internally in pregnancy and large amounts should not be taken regularly.

SUNFLOWER

Helianthus annuus. Cheerful sunflower faces can be seen peering over many an English garden wall in the summer, following the Sun on its daily journey. Despite their brash appearance, however, sunflowers are tender annuals. The seeds do not always germinate and when they do they don't always survive planting out, at the mercy of the weather and cats. Naturally, sunflowers need to be planted in full sun.

It is no surprise that it is the Sun that rules these bright, scruffy plants. Sunflower can be used magically to make wishes come true. Pick a flower at sunset, make your wish (nothing too outlandish!) and by the time the Sun has come round again your wish should have come true. It can also be used for fertility, wisdom and health. Sunflowers were cultivated by the American Indians 3,000 years ago and Aztec priestesses were adorned with them. They were introduced to Europe in the sixteenth century.

If you wish to know the truth about something cut a sunflower and place it under the bed while you sleep – with all the plants that have these nocturnal influences you could well end up with half the garden under your bed!

A woman who wishes to conceive should eat sunflower seeds – they are a tasty addition to nut roast! Medicinally the seeds have the power to relieve coughs and kidney troubles.

THYME

Thymus species. Another garden 'basic'; there are many varieties of thyme. It is an evergreen shrub that likes full sun. The thyme most usually used in cooking is the Mediterranean variety, but there are many other varieties, some lemon scented, some pine scented and with leaves of varying colours. Thyme is friendly to all plants growing nearby.

Thyme is ruled by Venus and gives courage, love, psychic gifts, health and sleep. One of the most appealing gifts of thyme, when worn, is the ability to see fairies. Take a sprig of thyme with you if you are going into a difficult situation and sniff it for courage – breathe in the vitality and powers of the herb. Thyme was used for embalming by the ancient Egyptians. Both the Greeks and Romans prized it, burning it to purify their temples and bathing in it for vigour and grace. Placed under your pillow, thyme will prevent nightmares, and carried it will increase your psychic powers.

Thyme is useful in the treatment of flatulence, coughs, laryngitis and diarrhoea.

VALERIAN

Valeriana officinalis. This hardly, herbaceous perennial may grow to 1.5 m and is happy in full sun, or light shade. It does not like its roots to be warm, but the reverse is true for the foliage. Its name derives from the same Latin root as valiant – *valere* – meaning 'to be strong'.

Valerian is ruled by Mercury, although some say Venus. Its magical powers include protection, purification, sleep-bringing and love. Canadian Indian warriors used to carry it in their medicine bags to use as an antiseptic on wounds. It was also prized by the Persians,

Chinese and Norsemen. A woman who wears a sprig of this plant on her clothes will find that men follow her, and the root is said to have been carried by the Pied Piper of Hamelin as the true attractant to the rats. Both the powdered root (which smells awful) and valerian sprigs can be used to ward danger away from the home. Valerian is used in incense.

Valerian has long been prized for its power to calm and balance. In the two World Wars it was again valued for treating resulting emotional traumas. Marion Green (in *The Magical Lore of Herbs*) says it is very valuable for easing pain and encouraging sleep. She continues:

> *Prepare by adding 1 oz powdered root to 1 pint cold water. Heat gently if wished. (Do not boil.) Alternatively place 1 level teaspoon of root in a cup of cold water and allow to stand all day. Take in doses of 1 wineglassful a couple of hours before retiring. For fits, convulsions, spasmodic pain, hysteria, 1 fluid ounce three or four times a day.*

(N.B. 1 oz = 28 g, 1 fl. oz = 28 ml approximately)

Valerian is also good for relieving cramps, tension headaches, period pains, sciatica and nervous symptoms caused by anxiety.

3

INCENSE

The scents I employ are spicy and aromatic; . . .
Sandal and cedar and Russian leather . . . the
sharp stimulus of frankincense, which is as if all
the trees in Paradise were burning.

Morgan Le Fay, from *Moon Magic* by Dion Fortune

*O*ne of the principal and most well-known magical uses of herbs is
*O*as incense, to be burnt in rites. Indeed, burning incense can be a
simple ritual in itself, if it is accompanied by visualisation and
affirmation. The evocative scent of incense is almost a prerequisite for
setting the scene for magic, and the spiralling smoke whispers of the
sacred, the secret and the realms of spirit. Candlelight and incense turn
an ordinary room into a den of enchantment.

It is most important to create the right atmosphere when doing magic. The subtle but potent plant essences released into the atmosphere as incense enable shifts in consciousness to take place gently. Besides this, they lend their own mysterious and specific energies to magical endeavour. Magicians have been said to call up demons in the incense vapour, using it to create an ephemeral body. However, the more simple rites of the 'craft of the wise' are concerned with practical matters and earth energies, of which there are few more arousing manifestations than incense, gentle though it is. Incense is also an excellent background to meditation and creative discussions, but it is inspirational rather than an aid to logic, so use it accordingly.

Herbs in incense

Incense is basically any combination of plant materials, mixed together and sprinkled on charcoal, to smoulder. Essential oils can also be used, and any part of the plant – root, bark, stem, petal, leaf – can be involved. Some plants smell quite different when burnt, and are not always pleasant, but incense doesn't have to smell 'nice' to be effective.

Whatever part of the world you live in, you can experiment with anything you find growing locally, drying it, cataloguing it and storing it for use in your spells. The romance and mystery of growing things all helps to increase our sense of true magic. You can be adventurous with this. Allow yourself to be guided by colours and any associations that occur. For instance, graceful willow branches look like trailing locks of hair, and an infusion of willow bark or leaves is good for treating dandruff. These willow tresses have a feminine look and the willow is ruled by the Moon and specifically linked to the witch goddess Hecate, and Persephone, Queen of the Underworld. In addition, the willow has associations with Ceres, goddess of crops and plants and mother to Persephone; with Artemis, goddess of the wild and untouchable and Hera, queen of the Olympian gods. Willow is used in healing, love and protective

magic, and anything specifically associated with Moon magic. Wands can be made from its wood.

Besides, certain plants only appear at specific times of the year, or are linked with it. Holly is associated with Yule, and is protective and lucky (ruled by Mars). You might like to burn holly bark or leaves as part of a spell against winter storms, for instance.

Marion Green (in *The Magical Lore of Herbs*) has this to say about incense ingredients:

> *Dried or fresh leaves and petals. Collect these as available. Dry carefully and store in glass jars. Keep away from light. Look out for red and white rose petals, flower heads from sweet smelling herbs like lavender, oregano, marjoram, rosemary, elder, borage, chamomile, rue, lemon balm.*

A very simple incense that you have gathered or grown yourself can be most poignant. Recently, at a barrow-mound in the Cotswolds where we had gone to watch the Sun penetrate into this specially constructed womb of earth, a companion ignited a sprig of sage and it was placed on a stone in the tunnel, as an offering. The moving moment when the depths of the earth glowed in welcome to the returning Sun was rendered unforgettable by this spicy scent. However, be careful when gathering plants unless your botanical knowledge is sound. Some plants are poisonous – for instance yew – so avoid anything of which you aren't sure.

In ancient times people would have had to be content with what they cultivated or found growing locally, and although there is something to be said for this, it is a shame to be so restricted when inspiring ingredients are readily come by. Finding and combining incense for an important spell can be fascinating and absorbing, and the enchantment begins and grows in the search. When using this more planned approach, start by noting both the planetary correspondences and the traditional magical uses of herbs that meet your purpose and take it from there, always following your own instincts if they speak strongly to you. As you handle and develop contact with these natural substances your 'magical consciousness' will take root and you will know what you are doing at a deep level.

Joss sticks

Incense, made from plant materials as described, is generally called raw incense. Ready-made incense that will burn by itself is also available and well known as joss sticks and incense cones. These are fine if you cannot readily obtain raw incense, and it is worthwhile finding some suitable joss sticks that you like (some do smell like old rope!). Joss sticks are sometimes named for the sign of the zodiac they are suited to, and that can be a good hint when choosing correspondences (although one can never be sure exactly what has been used in the making). Fragrances such as jasmine (Moon) and sandalwood (Sun) are also easily identified, but if something is labelled 'Aphrodisia' its constituents are uncertain, though it may smell lovely. Opinions vary on the importance of all this, however. For instance, some say that even synthetics work in magic, for, after all, nothing on this Earth can ever be truly 'synthetic' for all has come from the Earth initially. In this, as in most things, it is again best to be guided by your intuition.

Incense ingredients

As we have seen, there is a lot to be said for working with what you have grown, harvested and prepared yourself, or have gathered in nearby woods and fields. Rae Beth, author of *Hedge Witch*, says that she generally burns pine in winter and lavender in summer, unless a specific rite calls for something more complex, and there is an attractive simplicity to this.

If you wish for more complex blends, however, or are interested in 'dabbling', growing and preparing your own may not be practical. Besides, incense without the more exotic gum resins isn't nearly as rich. Incense ingredients can be bought from suppliers – see 'Suppliers' at the back of this book – and there is no reason why herbs and spices shouldn't be bought from health food shops and the ethnic stores that sometimes have beautiful spices, generally for use in curries, at low prices. You can send away for ingredients, but

enquire before you buy from the supplier about the standards used in growing the produce. Some favour wild, organic and home-grown herbs, and observe the phase of the Moon while gathering. I think it is best to avoid supermarket produce generally (although if you already have something in your spice rack it may be silly to avoid using it, economy being a consideration!). Proprietary herbs are grown to a high standard for culinary use, but their cultivation is often far from 'natural'. Besides, supermarkets are unmagical places, with the merciless glare of their lighting and the jittery energies of irritated shoppers infesting in the air! The basil or cinnamon you intend to use for incense for your love spell just isn't quite the same when chosen under those circumstances.

It is possible to buy ready-blended incense, both from suppliers and from many 'New Age' shops. These incense blends are often beautiful and are named after planets, goddesses and gods, seasonal festivals for which they are suitable, etc. There is no substitute for the satisfaction of blending your own, however, and this gives you the conviction that you have done your magical 'job' properly, from the basic level upwards. Creating your own blend is just like deriving a simple recipe, and some examples will be given later in this chapter, together with a selection of incense ingredients, mostly from my own 'bank'. I have chosen most of these because they are fairly inexpensive, but I do include the gum resins frankincense, myrrh, copal and benzoin, because I think they are worth the investment.

Burning incense

Incense is burnt on charcoal that has been ignited and placed in a heatproof container. This can be a bowl half-filled with salt or sand. A censer is possibly the best vessel as it is easier to waft the incense smoke around, but the metal will get hot. A saucer won't do for it will also get too hot. Charcoal and container can usually be bought where you obtain the incense.

So, for incense burning you need incense, a heatproof container, knife or tongs, charcoal, matches and a candle or taper. Burning

incense isn't always as easy as it sounds, and charcoal can be difficult to handle. The best practical instructions I have seen on this are given by Shan in *Circlework*. She says:

> *Open the silver foil of the [charcoal] packet, and take one brick out. If you can store the packet in an airtight jar. Have the container ready to hand.*
>
> *Matches do light charcoal, but it's a great deal easier with a taper, or spare candle. Hold the brick in thumb and forefinger on one side, put the other side in the flame. Hold it there until sparks start spitting off it – they won't hurt you.*
>
> *Keep holding the brick in the flame after the sparks start, until they start to move away from the edge of the disc towards your fingers holding it! The sparks move quite slowly, though. The part that is alight behind the sparks goes blacker.*
>
> *Now put the brick down on the sand or earth, upright like a wheel, standing on the part that's sparking. This will draw the fire up through the rest.*
>
> *If the sparks stop before their advancing line reaches the other side of the disc, put the flame to it again . . .*
>
> *Once the brick has burnt through, the sparks stop. Knock it over flat, with its little hollow all ready to act as a cup for the incense. The other side is flat.*
>
> *It's now very hot so don't touch it with your hands. Tweezers are useful, or a spoon or pocket knife.*

Now your charcoal is ready to use, so place a pinch of incense in the hollow and watch the bewitching swirls transform your room, as the aroma penetrates deep into your most secret and intuitional recesses. The magical work is beginning! You can top up the incense as often as you feel necessary – about every ten to fifteen minutes, and one block will burn for about an hour. After your purpose is finished dispose of the remains with great care as they may still be hot, and you don't want to start a fire.

STORING AND CATALOGUING YOUR INGREDIENTS

Herbs for incense should be stored in airtight jars, away from heat, light or damp. I have collected dark glass jars that originally contained tea granules. Label each jar clearly with the name of the ingredient and its planetary correspondence.

It is important to obtain your own impression of the incense ingredient so that it may really become part of your fantasy and creative world. To do this, place yourself in a light trance, as described in Chapter 1, burn a pinch of the single ingredient and note any impressions, memories, feelings, pictures that come into your mind. Write these in a special notebook (an address book can be good, as it is already marked alphabetically) beside the name of the herb. After you have done this look up the magical and other meanings in this book, or in one of the books in the bibliography. You may be surprised how often your impressions harmonise with the traditional correspondences. Even if they do not, they are equally valuable so take them into account when choosing herbs to blend for an incense.

INCENSE FOR MAGICAL PURPOSES

Spells have a purpose, and this needs to be defined and categorised when choosing incense ingredients. Magical goals can be aligned with one or more astrological correspondence, which makes it simple to create recipes. However, as always your feelings about a particular herb may encourage you to use it somewhat differently – for instance, burning juniper berries evokes for me freedom and faraway places. Juniper is ruled by the Sun, but my reaction is more akin to the characteristics of Jupiter or Mercury, and so I may bear that in mind when using the berries.

MAGICAL GOALS AND CORRESPONDENCES

Courage   Mars, Sun (sometimes Venus, surprisingly)
Happiness   Moon, Venus, Sun, Jupiter
Healing   Moon mainly, also Venus, Sun, Mars, Mercury (depending on what type)
Legal matters   Sun, Jupiter
Love   Moon, Venus, Mars for passion and sexuality
Luck   Sun, Jupiter, Venus
Lust   Mars, Saturn
Money   Sun, Jupiter, Saturn, Venus
Peace   Venus, Moon
Protection   Saturn, Sun, Mars
Psychic awareness   Moon, Jupiter, Mercury (divination), Saturn (sometimes for visions)
Purification   Mercury, Moon, Sun, Saturn, Mars for expunging

The above is only a rough guide, as herbs have their own special affinities in tradition and folklore that don't always tie in with their astrological rulership. For instance, lavender, ruled by Mercury, promotes happiness. So below is a further list, using the herbs from the 'bank' given on pages 48–50 and also essential oils in Chapter 4. These should cover most of your magical goals.

MAGICAL GOALS AND HERBS AND OILS

Courage   Dragon's blood, frankincense, geranium (oil)
Happiness   Lavender (oil), St John's wort
Healing   Calamus, juniper, lemon balm, rose, sandalwood, oils of peppermint, eucalyptus and coriander
Love   Clove (oil), copal, coriander (oil), dragon's blood, juniper, lavender (oil), lemon balm, orange (oil), orris, peppermint (oil), rose, vervain, ylang-ylang (oil)

Luck   Calamus, orange (oil), rose

Lust   Clove (oil), patchouli (oil), peppermint (oil)

Money   Calamus, clove (oil), galangal, orange (oil), patchouli (oil), vervain

Peace   Lavender (oil), cumin

Protection   Calamus, clove (oil), copal, cypress (oil), dragon's blood, eucalyptus (oil), frankincense, galangal, juniper, lavender (oil), myrrh, orris, patchouli (oil), rose, vervain, wormwood

Psychic awareness   Clove (oil), galangal, mace, orange, orris, peppermint (oil), rose, wormwood

Purification   Benzoin, calamus, copal, eucalyptus (oil), frankincense, lavender, myrrh, peppermint (oil), sandalwood, valerian, vervain

N.B. Where I have stated 'oil' this does not mean that the oil **should** be used but that the characteristics are more fully described in Chapter 4. With the exception of ylang-ylang the dried herb version is available, and is really preferable, for oils are concentrated and you may find it easier to 'balance' your recipe if all the ingredients are dry.

I have omitted the more usual culinary herbs as they are well known – for instance, everyone knows ginger is 'hot', and it is no surprise to find it is ruled by Mars. However, you can raid your spice rack to use these herbs magically, and they deserve a mention.

Properties of culinary herbs

Basil   Ruled by Mars, hot and hearty. Used in love/lust spells.

Bay   Ruled by the Sun, strong and rich. Burned to expel negativity, protect, purify and induce visions.

Cinnamon   Ruled by the Sun, this is sweet and stimulating and is said to raise spirituality. Also good for money, healing, protection, lust and love.

Ginger   Ruled by Mars, hot. Lends power to spells.

Marjoram (oregano)   Ruled by Mercury, lively and tangy. Used in love spells, but I haven't tried it in incense.

Mint   Ruled by Venus, although I link it also with Mercury, this clean, fresh herb is used for healing.

Parsley   Sharp and tangy, ruled by Mercury. Not often used in incense.

Rosemary   Ruled by the Sun, warm and strong. A very ancient incense ingredient, purifying, positive, healing and youth-giving. Can be used as a substitute for frankincense.

Sage   Ruled by Jupiter, although some say Venus, this is hearty and fragrant. Protects, purifies, promotes long life and wisdom.

Thyme   Ruled by Venus, this is sweet and spicy. Also used for cleansing, good health and courage.

BLENDING INCENSE

Some say that herbs for use in magic should not come in contact with certain metals, but others use a 'white-handled knife', one of the traditional tools. I think scissors are more efficient for cutting herbs, but you may prefer to pinch them off between finger-nail and thumb. Remember to ask the plant if you may take some of it. I usually rub the tip of my thumb over the broken stem as a gesture of healing and thanks. Plants are deeply identified with the cycle of death and resurrection that is manifest in Nature, and there is an air of trust and acceptance about them. Nonetheless, we should not take them for granted.

Use a pestle and mortar for crushing dried ingredients, not an electric grinder. I'm all for labour-saving technology, but not for magical purposes. As you prepare your incense, allow your mind to dwell on the purpose for which it will be used – try not to be tense, thinking about shopping or your long day at the office. When preparing a blend – say for protection – visualise this specific purpose and let your energies flow into the herbs. Mix up blends in a jar large enough to shake all the ingredients about, and add oils one or two drops at a time, shaking in between to disperse the oil – otherwise it will cling to a few grains only. Then transfer your blend to a suitable jar for storage.

It is easy to make your own blends. For instance, a happiness incense could consist of lavender, St John's wort and dried orange

peel. This would be for an 'invigorating' types of happiness. To combat stress we might substitute rose petals for the orange, or to banish strife, cumin. You can experiment and see how you feel. My blends, given below, are ones that I like and have found effective, but they are not necessarily 'right' in any crystallised fashion. Experiment and find out for yourself.

Suggested ingredients Larder

These are chosen for no special reason, other than because they cover a reasonable spectrum of magical characteristics, and are mostly inexpensive and easy to obtain. Consult the books listed in 'Further Reading' to explore more ingredients.

Benzoin   Ruled by the Sun and associated with Leo, Aquarius and the element of air. This is powerful, expunging and means business. Used for success, energy, magical power, purification and astral projection.

Calamus   Ruled by the Moon and linked with Cancer and Pisces, this is sweet and peaceful. Used for purification, protection, money, luck and healing.

Cedar   Ruled by the Sun and associated with the signs Aries and Sagittarius. Fragrant, purifying smoke, used also for money, health and protection.

Copal   Ruled by the Sun and associated with Aries, Leo and Sagittarius, the vapour of copal speaks of heart's ease and is clear and uplifting. Used magically for protection, purification, exorcism, spirituality and love.

Cumin   Ruled by Mars and known as a curry ingredient this is penetrating and spicy. Used for protection, exorcism, fidelity and against theft.

Dragon's blood   Ruled by Mars, this is a palm-tree resin, and expensive in the United Kingdom. It is powerful, speaking of crashing flames and lightning. Use it for courage, love, protection

and exorcism. It gives sexual energy and adds potency to all spells. I associate it especially with the energies of menstruation which can be used for power in magic.

Marion Green (in *The Magical Lore of Herbs*) gives an interesting spell using dragon's blood that she says she found in an old family notebook. She tried it once and it worked. So, if you wish to call your lover to you, perform this spell on a Friday evening – Friday is sacred to Venus. You must check the position of the Moon in an ephemeris or planetary tables, for the spell must be done when the Moon is in Taurus or Libra (both Venus-ruled signs). You will need a coal fire, or just your hot charcoal in your incense burner. Marion says:

> *Think carefully of your intent. Throw three pinches of dragon's blood on to your fire, calling your lover's name while you do so. He or she should be with you within twenty-four hours. Incidentally, the resin will flare when thrown into the heat, so be prepared.*

Frankincense   Ruled by the Sun and linked to Aries, Sagittarius and Leo, this is rich and royal. It is a 'must' for the incense 'larder'. Use it for protection, purification, spirituality, exorcism and courage.

Galangal   Ruled by Mars, this is a hot one. If unavailable, ginger is a substitute. Used for protection, health, lust, money, psychic powers and breaking hexes (evil spells).

Juniper   Ruled by the Sun and speaking (to me) of freedom and romance, this herb is used for protection, healing, love and exorcism. It helps psychic powers and is an ancient incense ingredient.

Lemon balm   Ruled by the Moon, this has a clean, healthy aroma. It is used for healing, fertility, sleep, prophecy, gardening, love, peace and compassion.

Mace   Ruled by Mercury and associated with Virgo and Gemini, this has an enlivening effect and is used to increase psychic powers and sharpen the intellect.

Myrrh   Ruled by the Moon, or perhaps the planet of passage Pluto, this is another 'must'. It speaks of laying to rest, mourning

and resurrection. Used in embalming myrrh brings a feeling of 'gathering gloom' as the Christmas carol says, but it is also peaceful. It is linked to Scorpio, Cancer and Pisces and is used for purification, exorcism, spirituality and protection.

Orris root Ruled by Venus, and so associated with Libra and Taurus, this speaks of peace and detachment and is used for love, protection, psychic awareness and divination.

Rose petals Ruled by Venus and linked to Taurus, Libra and Cancer, this conveys love, beauty and pleasure. Used for protection, psychic awareness, prophetic dreams, luck, healing, and – of course – love.

Sandalwood I have noticed this linked to the Sun and the Moon. It is warm and protective, linked to Cancer, Pisces and Leo and used for purification, spirituality, protection, healing, exorcism, and astral projection. However, sandalwood has been over-used and the trees are becoming scarce. Cedar may be a substitute, although I cannot say what may be the pros and cons of using this. However, there could be no harm in using twigs, as some American Indians do in sweat baths.

Valerian Ruled by Mars or Mercury, the herbalist Culpeper gives it to the latter, and that feels appropriate to me. The odour is a bit like stale sweat, but if you can get beyond that to what it evokes, it seems to me to speak of freedom and journeys of the spirit, and it is used for protection, purification, love and sleep.

Vervain Ruled by Venus, this has links with Taurus, Virgo and Capricorn. It has an aura of earthy mysteries, and I also link it to the Crone aspect of the Triple Goddess. (This is described fully in *Witchcraft – a beginner's guide* in this series.) It is used for protection, purification, money and love.

Wormwood Ruled by Mars this is fairly pungent! Linked to Aries and Scorpio it is used for psychic awareness and protection.

Of course this is only a tiny representation of all the available herbs for incense. You may notice that Saturn and Jupiter are poorly represented, but the former is catered for in the beautiful oils patchouli and cypress, and the latter in clove oil and sage. Any herb associated with Saturn is also associated with Aquarius, for it was the old 'ruler' of Aquarius, before Uranus was discovered. The

versatile oil of lavender is linked to Mercury, Virgo and Gemini. Mercury is 'exalted' in Aquarius, (according to some writers) and so any Mercury herb may be linked to Aquarius. Jupiter rules Sagittarius and is the old ruler of Pisces.

SUGGESTED BLENDS

Banishing   (anything negative; this is strong)   Benzoin, wormwood, myrrh

Banishing   (much more gentle, for domestic and psychological matters)   Myrrh, frankincense, copal

Fire of Azrael incense   for general psychism given in Dion Fortune's novel *The Sea Priestess*   Sandalwood, cedar, juniper

General incense   for all rituals and to purify the area (given by Scott Cunningham) three parts frankincense, two parts myrrh, one part cinnamon

In honour of the Crone aspect of the Goddess   Vervain, myrrh, cypress

In honour of the Maiden aspect of the Goddess   Vervain, lavender, rose

In honour of the Mother aspect of the Goddess   Rose, frankincense, cypress

In honour of the Horned God   Sandalwood, myrrh, patchouli

Healing   Rosemary, juniper and myrrh

Love   Geranium, rose petals, copal – for more sensual and 'spunky' love add dragon's blood, cinnamon and patchouli

Full Moon   Frankincense, sandalwood, rose petals

Dark Moon   Myrrh, cypress, orris

Prosperity   Frankincense, cinnamon, lemon balm, mace, orange peel, copal

Protection   (given by Scott Cunningham) two parts frankincense, one part sandalwood, one half part rosemary

Psychic vision   Frankincense, bay, wormwood (this smells better if there is a preponderance of frankincense)

To purify the atmosphere   Pine, juniper, and cedar is suggested by Rae Beth in *Hedge Witch*

Rituals

Basic cleansing ritual, using incense alone

As an example, if we wish to cleanse an object for use in magic, we may burn an incense of the appropriate constituents, and hold the object in the smoke. Then we could move the object around in an anticlockwise circle, three times, saying something like:

> 'Cleansed be, safe be,
> Any badness leave thee'

Suitable incense ingredients for this ritual might be copal, benzoin, frankincense, myrrh, sandalwood and vervain.

This simple rite might be suitable for objects such as crystals, or new implements bought for use in magic, as meditation aids or similar. If we buy something from a junk shop, such as a cauldron, we may prefer to conduct a more complex rite in order to feel sure that it is thoroughly cleansed of all the many influences that would have come in contact with it in its existence.

After cleansing it is often a good idea to leave an important object in the light of the Full Moon for a few hours, or you may prefer simply to hold it between your hands, close your eyes and affirm that it is now a valuable aid to your endeavours. You may visualise it glowing with the light of purity, and welcome it, mentally, to your array of special objects.

Spell for self-confidence

Incense blend   Frankincense, benzoin, dragon's blood, mace, orange peel, rose petals

Preferably choose a time just before Full Moon. Form your magic circle and be very still. Imagine warmth within you, gathering behind your navel and gradually spreading outwards so the whole of your body feels warm and glowing.

Light a golden yellow candle and say:

> 'May my inner confidence glow like this candle flame.
> May it be an ever-burning flame inside me
> May it grow like the Moon and, having reached fullness,
> remain constant as the Northern Star.
> As this candle burns and is transformed, so my
> inner confidence becomes complete.
> So shall it be.'

When you are ready, close down your ritual and your psychic centres consciously and thoroughly. You may put the candle somewhere safe to burn out or relight it each day until it is finished.

PRACTICE

Truly, the only way to feel at home with incense materials is to try them yourself. You may start immediately if you have some materials to hand – just use what you have at first, while you are experimenting. Or you may prefer to be more organised and make a 'shopping list' for a blend you plan to use.

There is no mystery to preparing incense – it is very simple. And yet there is a mystery to using it effectively. You will discover this as you explore.

The way to health is to have an aromatic bath and scented massage every day.

Hippocrates, the father of medicine' c.460–377 BCE, as quoted by Daniele Ryman in *The Aromatherapy Handbook*

*E*ssential oils are oils or essences extracted from plants, sometimes from the wood, the root, the flower, leaf or seed. For example, in the case of lavender, the oil comes from the glands found on the hairs covering stem, leaf and flower. Oils are extracted by steam distillation, pressing or solvent extraction, depending on what is appropriate to the particular plant. They possess an immense array of special properties that are magical in themselves.

Essential oils are sold in small glass bottles, each usually containing 10 ml. Oils should always be bought from a supplier you can trust, such as a Natural Therapy centre, or specialist supplier (see 'Suppliers'), so that you can be sure to avoid synthetics. At first the choice may seem bewildering, but you will soon get to know the oils you like. A 'library' of essential oils will be given later in this chapter, along with their uses and planetary correspondences. Oils vary greatly in price and I have restricted discussion mostly to inexpensive oils. After a while you may like to experiment with others. Depending on your funds you may like to build up your stock gradually. Remember not to sniff too many oils in succession, for after three or four your sense of smell will be less acute and the subtle nuances may be lost.

You can use essential oils to treat a wide variety of ailments by virtue of massage and the wonderful effects of scent – for our sense of smell is the most acute of our senses and has a 'hotline' to the unconscious mind. This is properly called aromatherapy, and the true practice of it requires considerable training. Oils can be used to purify the system, ease digestive complaints and skin problems, improve circulation, help relieve asthma and bronchitis and many more conditions. They also have potent effects on the nervous system, emotions and moods. Oils are easily absorbed by the skin. If you wish to explore this in more detail you can start with some of the books in 'Further Reading'. In this chapter we shall look at some basic ways of using oils, therapeutically and magically, so you can get started on your exploration of one of Nature's most exciting and precious gifts.

OiL BURNERS

An easy way to get to know and enjoy your oils is by using an oil burner. These are becoming popular and are available in all sorts of shapes and sizes and beautiful designs, but again care needs to be taken when selecting your burner.

Oil burners have two compartments, one underneath to hold the candle or nightlight, and a small bowl above in which you put the water and essential oil. Not all burners are well designed, for some have the flame too close to the upper bowl. This means the water boils and evaporates and the oil burns on the bottom, smelling lovely and 'incensy' for a while, but it means your expensive oil is gone all too soon and your burner may crack.

The best burners leave about 4 to 5 cm between the flame and the base of the upper bowl – take the depth of the nightlight into consideration here. Shop around for a burner you like, for the cheapest isn't always the best. Your oil burner, with its flickering candle flame will be a focal point in a dimly lit room as you relax, do magic, massage or begin to make love – for essential oils set the mood for love beautifully.

Instructions often come with the better oil burners. Generally, half-fill the upper bowl of the burner with water and sprinkle on it between seven and twelve drops of oil – obviously the oil will float and evaporate as the water heats. Each 10 ml bottle contains about 200 drops of oil, so giving you about 20 'burnings'. The fragrance should last for an hour or longer, and in an enclosed space it may linger for a day, as there will be a residue left in the bowl when all the water has evaporated.

Oil burners can help create magical effects. They are less pungent than incense, less prone to cause headaches and more acceptable to people who are uneasy about ritual, for they can be ordinary household objects. I find them versatile and more easy to use than incense, although for powerful rites there is no substitute for proper incense and its spiralling smoke.

ḊILUTION of OILS

Always be careful when handling oils as they are strong substances and will burn eyes or sensitive parts of your body! Use glass bottles (never plastic, for the oil will react with the plastic) and keep

everything clean. If you spill any wipe it up immediately with a tissue, and avoid getting undiluted oils on your skin.

For massage, the oils are diluted in what are called carrier oils. These are vegetable oils with no scent of their own. Only use pure, cold-pressed oils and never mineral oil (i.e. baby oil). Carrier oils can usually be purchased where you buy the essential oil, and are less expensive. Two of the best are sweet almond and grapeseed oil.

Dilute in the proportion of two drops per teaspoon (5 ml) but make this weaker for use on the face or for young children. It is best to make up only the amount you are going to use, but in practice I find blends do keep for many weeks. This may not always be the case, however, so add 5 per cent wheatgerm oil to your mixture to prevent it from going off. However, this won't be necessary if you use jojoba oil as your carrier oil.

Store blends somewhere cool and dark. This applies equally to essential oils themselves. Keep them somewhere dry – not in bathroom or kitchen – away from heat and light. It is best to have a special box for your oils. When you take the lid off, the exciting fragrance gets you in the mood for using and exploring them.

Essential oils should never be ingested as this could be dangerous; enough of the essence is absorbed through smell and by the skin to make this unnecessary. Keep your oils away from children and animals.

Massage

Massage is an eloquent way of expressing care and giving healing. Anyone with some sensitivity can massage, so rely on your instincts and the responses of your subject. Massage is both stimulating and calming, and you can choose oils appropriate to your purpose. Some people like firm, almost rough manipulation, whereas others prefer it to be gentle. Naturally this will also depend on the part of the body you are touching and what the ailment – if any – may be. Again, to

explore this further you may like to read some of the books on aromatherapy listed in 'Further Reading' or enrol on a massage course.

Use common sense when massaging. Don't massage where there is a swelling, deep pain in the joints or a fracture or dislocation. Don't massage a recent scar or anywhere inflamed, or where the skin is broken, or over varicose veins. It is best not to massage people who have a temperature. Be sensitive to the responses of your subject, and get advice from a doctor, osteopath or chiropractor for serious conditions. In short, when in doubt about massage – don't. You may still transfer healing energies simply by laying your hands on the affected area, and you can benefit from the therapy of scent by using an oil burner, placed nearby.

healing energies

Healing magic is some of the easiest to perform, for people naturally want to get better, and most of us love to heal. The power of belief and trust on the part of the patient is a major part of the process. However, partly because belief can be so potent you should take great care with this sort of healing. Sometimes belief in the healer can mask important symptoms until it is too late to treat by other means, and this could have consequences that are literally fatal. Healing can indeed work on terminal cases and there are documented accounts of this, but you need to be clear what you are up against and have the involvement of qualified medical practitioners. I include here acupuncturists and homoeopaths as well as doctors. The last certainly shouldn't be avoided by those who prefer more alternative therapies, for a good doctor can embody the healing archetype (often without realising it) and there is always a role for medicines, antibiotics and surgery, although these can be greatly overplayed. The luckiest patient is the one who has a doctor and alternative practitioner who respect each other and are willing to work together to achieve a cure, for each may have something to offer.

For anything but the mildest complaints, get the symptoms checked out with a doctor first. Doctors often prescribe antibiotics for comparatively minor problems because they are expected to, and are pleasantly surprised if the patient declines. For instance, I preferred to treat an attack of tonsilitis in my ten-year-old son by healing, rest, sage infusion and honey – but I checked with the doctor to be sure my son didn't have meningitis. We had our prescription as a precaution, but we never collected the tablets. My son was back at school in two days.

Your healing energies can be easily activated. Make sure that you and the patient are in a peaceful, comfortable place, and that the patient is settled in a relaxed position, usually lying or sitting. Make sure also that you won't be disturbed. The light should be dim – candles are best – and the fragrance of a suitable oil or combination of oils should pervade the atmosphere from your oil burner. (You may choose your oil from those listed in this chapter.)

If you have learnt how to open your chakras – see Chapter 1 – do so now. Draw the life-force up through each of the chakras so that it issues from your crown in a fountain, like a Roman candle. Now circulate the energy so that it re-enters the solar plexus chakra from the fountain, rises, circulates, re-enters and so you are 'humming' like a battery. When you are ready you may direct this energy up from your solar plexus chakra and down your arms into your hands. You may feel them radiating warmth. Visualise this golden, healing energy entering your patient, warming, healing and envigorating him or her. See the hurt disappearing. If you now massage it is unlikely that you will be able to keep up the visualisation uninterrupted, so keep reminding yourself of the golden light and re-affirming this energy flow. When you have finished, remember to close down properly for your own protection. You shouldn't feel depleted, for healing is a two-way thing, but you may be a little tired. A bite to eat will boost your blood sugar and ensure the chakras are closed.

Where there is pain it may be better to imagine the healing energy as green or blue – follow your intuition here. Some healers flick away pain with the left hand, imagining it as flecks of leaden grey or angry

red. So you may give healing with your positive hand (usually the right in right-handed people) and take away pain with the negative hand (the left in right-handed people). Direct the negative 'vibes' away from your own body and let them be absorbed into the great body of Mother Earth, who will have no trouble neutralising them.

If you find that you have somehow taken the pain into yourself and are feeling awful, stop doing this kind of healing until you have done more work with magic and visualisation and are better able to protect yourself. If it should happen that you do a lot of healing, whether in this way or professionally, as a nurse or counsellor for instance, you will need support from colleagues and friends and you will need to know how to look after yourself. This is too often neglected, to the cost of practitioners and patients.

Healing energies often flow especially well between parent and child or loving partners. I have seen quite nasty injuries heal and go away in a couple of days with this method of touch and visualisation, but I repeat, when in any doubt always check with a doctor.

Selected essential oils

CARDAMOM

Cardamom seeds are a fragrant curry ingredient. Tangy and spicy, magical uses are lust and love and the rulership is Venus, which I find surprising as the plants come from the ginger family, which is ruled by Mars, and the aroma is potent. Cardamom is supposed to be an excellent remedy for flatulence and a tonic to the nerves and heart.

CLOVE

Sharp and spicy, this is ruled by Jupiter. If one can get away from the apples-and-country-kitchen associations, this scent has an 'arrow-like' quality that recalls the symbolism of Sagittarius – explorative

sign of the Archer, ruled by Jupiter. Clove oil is a strong antiseptic and is especially good for digestive infections. It keeps away moths and wasps, and a drop of the essential oil applied directly to a tooth cavity is said to take away toothache. Some people find that the scent of clove reminds them of the dentist – a rather unglamorous association and not so appealing! Magical uses include protection, money and love.

CORIANDER

Warm and wonderfully aromatic, this is ruled by Mars and I especially link it to Scorpio. Magically it can be used for healing and love. Coriander seeds are an ingredient in curries. It is a stimulant to the digestive system, and being warm and antispasmodic it is good for relieving rheumatism and pains in the joints.

CYPRESS

Ruled by Saturn, also associated with Capricorn and Virgo. Rich, woody, earthy, secret and wise. May also be associated with Pluto and therefore Scorpio. Also the dark of the Moon. Associated with funerals and said to ease grief. Used magically and emotionally to confer protection, to give security, connection with the Earth, calm in crisis, solace in grief, and to encourage an understanding of the Earth Elemental Spirits. Medically good as an astringent and anti-spasmodic; good for treating coughs, excessive perspiration and period problems.

Use cypress oil in your burner or as massage when your period is heavy or if you have a congested chest. If you feel hyped-up and jittery, insecure, sad or anxious, or if you feel you have lost your way emotionally or mentally, use cypress oil for a grounding, protective effect. This will be especially potent during those few days around New Moon, when she is invisible – the dark of the Moon. Your calendar or diary should tell you when this is. Many women have their periods at the dark of the Moon, or at Full Moon.

eucalyptus

Ruled by the Moon and Saturn, this is a therapeutic oil, partaking of
the Moon's healing powers and Saturn's firmness and stability. This
tree and its oil are also associated with Cancer, Pisces and Scorpio.
It is used magically for purification, protection and healing. I
imagine ancient temples of healing and meditation storing
eucalyptus leaves, from which the oil is extracted. This may not be
far from the truth, for before the Bronze Age secular and sacred were
united and harvest produce was often stored in temples and
overseen by priestesses and priests.

Eucalyptus is good for combating respiratory problems and catarrh.
For 'flu, chesty coughs and colds add between six and ten drops to a
warm bath – this is also good for rheumatism – and soak for 10 to
15 minutes. (If you have 'flu ensure the water isn't too hot or you
could feel faint. Make sure the bathroom is warm, wrap up warmly
as soon as you are dry and return to bed.) If you are running the
bath for someone else you can direct healing energies into the water
with the method described above.

As a healing spell for someone who is sick, rub a green candle with
eucalyptus oils, saying:

> 'Hale and hearty,
> By my spell,
> . . . . (person's name)
> Is whole and well.'

Visualise the person as completely well, not 'getting better'. Light the
candle and affirm that as the flame transforms the wax so illness is
totally transformed to health. You may let the candle burn
completely, or relight it daily, until it is burnt out.

frankincense

This is a majestic oil which I include because it is lovely, although
expensive. Ruled by the Sun, frankincense protects and aids

spirituality. Therapeutically it is also protective, and can be helpful in dealing with stress, meditating or concentrating. Also good for treating respiratory problems.

GERANIUM

Ruled by Venus, this oil is heady and sweet. It is also associated with Taurus, and to some extent Libra. Magically it is used for love, happiness, protection and courage. Use it to ensure the affections of your lover remain constant. It is good for treating skin inflammations and dermatitis, as a sedative when anxious and an anti-depressant also – dilute as specified above for massage.

LAVENDER

Ruled by Mercury, lavender is fresh, clean and envigorating. It is also associated with Gemini, Virgo and Aquarius. Magically it is used for cleansing, protection, peace, love and happiness. Therapeutically it has many uses, as an anti-depressant, for recurring infections, muscular and joint pains and sunburn. I have known lavender placed in an oil burner to dispel the most stubborn headache. Be careful, however. Some people say that oil burners give them a headache. In this case the oil should be diluted in cold water (two drops per teaspoon) and saturated cotton-wool pressed to the temples. (N.B. The oil will not dissolve in water as it does in oil.)

Lavender is also good for relieving stings. Extract the sting with tweezers if it is still present, bathe the area with lemon juice or vinegar and apply lavender, diluted as for headache. During a recent hot summer my baby was stung three times by wasps. With the above treatment administered immediately he hardly cried and had almost no redness or swelling. Lavender oil can be used neat for stings and burns, but I fear this may be too strong for some skins and have not tried it.

Burn oil of lavender while you study to keep a clear head and concentration.

MYRRH

Another expensive oil, but irresistible. It is secret, musky and rather bitter. Ruled by the Moon, myrrh is associated also with the sign of Scorpio, as well as Cancer and Pisces. Magically used for protection, purification and spirituality, since ancient times, myrrh has been used in religious rites. The ancient Egyptians used it in their embalming methods. Therapeutically it is said to be anti-inflammatory and good for acne and dermatitis. For treating this it may be diluted in soya oil two to four drops to two teaspoons of soya.

ORANGE

This fresh and envigorating oil is ruled by the Sun, and also associated with Leo and Sagittarius. Its magical uses are for psychic awareness, love, luck and divination. It is good for combating digestive upsets, poor appetite and constipation. It also lends a feeling of energy and optimism and its fragrance may help in making decisions. If you really can't make up your mind about something, take a bath with half a dozen drops of orange oil in it (be careful not to use too much, as this oil can be an irritant). Relax and try not to think about your problem. As you towel dry you may find the decision has made itself in your mind.

PATCHOULI

Mossy, earthy and sensual, patchouli was described to me as evocative of 1960s 'flower power' by an aromatherapist who didn't look old enough to remember – due possibly to her constant use of beneficial oils! Patchouli is ruled by Saturn, and linked to Capricorn, Aquarius, Taurus and Virgo. Magically it is good for protection, lust and money. Use it in your burner for grounding, practicality and common sense. A few drops can be added to shampoo for oily hair. Patchouli is good for skin that is beginning to age and has anti-inflammatory properties that help with sores.

PEPPERMINT

Mars and Mercury are both said to rule this sharp and stimulating plant, and it is associated with Aries, Gemini, Virgo, Aquarius and Scorpio. The botanical name is *Mentha piperita* as distinct from spearmint (*Mentha viridis*) which Culpeper says is ruled by Venus. It can be used in magic for purification, protection, psychic awareness, lust, money, healing, love and exorcism – an awful lot contained within an inexpensive little bottle! It is good for relieving flatulence, intestinal pains and nausea (but use with caution in pregnancy, and do not use in the first 16 weeks, as it is too stimulating – this is not a remedy for 'morning sickness'). One of its nicest uses is as a footbath, and if you have a bidet you may put it to the traditional British use by adding a few drops of peppermint oil to the water and soaking those poor, tired feet. If you don't have a bidet a bowl will do just as well, of course.

ROSEWOOD

This tree is ruled by Venus and I link it with Taurus and Libra. Magically it is used for reconciliation, calming and peace. Therapeutically, it balances the nerves and dispels an inclination to daydream. Try burning a mixture of peppermint, lavender and rosewood when studying to help concentration and keep the mind clear and retentive.

Rosewood grows in the Amazonian rainforests and tragically huge amounts have been chopped down to be used mainly as chopsticks. Because of this we should not really use the oil. As a substitute try ho-wood, from Japan, which is said to be similar in composition, and is not much more expensive.

YLANG-YLANG

This langourous, sensual oil is again ruled by Venus and linked to Taurus, Libra, Pisces and possibly Scorpio. Magically we can use it

for love and the stabilisation of emotions. It is good for treating shock and frustration and for regulating the heart rate. Burn it in the bedroom if there are any types of sexual dysfunction, or to aid the elimination and healing of jealousy and resentment. Like music it has 'charms to soothe the savage breast'.

PRACTICE

The above is a small selection of essential oils. To get to know and love them please experiment for yourself. Try them out in a burner or as a massage. You can massage yourself if you have no one to practise on, but obviously this is better done in a pair. Try massaging your abdomen, shoulders or feet. Note the effects and impressions of the oils upon you and record them in your special notebook.

5

MORE ABOUT
SPELLS AND RITES

A Sage Tea, for the Mind.

The gray-leaved sage
Stands fresh and fine
When even trees
Fall prey to time;
Pluck its growth,
Brew an infusion
Against all darkness
And confusion;
Drink its strength,
With these words:

'Sage make green
The winter rain:
Charm the demon
From my brain.'

Valerie Worth, *The Crone's Book of Words*

*M*aking a spell involves imagination and concentration. It means *'spelling out'* your intention. Natural substances are generally best for use in spells, as these hold magical 'charge' more effectively. More than this, natural substances are harmonious to humans and they have ways of speaking straight to the subconscious. All things have a language, stones hold secrets, herbs and oils have a silent song and trees are magical symphonies. These are truths we have lost sight of and we are the poorer for this.

Spellcraft

People are apt to think spells are devices to get them what they want, and although many are superficially sceptical they secretly hope that it will work. Of course a spell is to 'get you what you want', but it also has a vital element of mysticism and worship. Handling stones and oils, weaving threads, making potions – all these are an act of adoration of the Mother Goddess, an affirmation of our roots and our essence. The greatest magic is always a feeling of union with the Mother Goddess. However, in moving in these realms we certainly are able to get results, for we are also mobilising the powers of our mind and being, and harmonising with natural forces.

Some people say magic will work only for a need, but then we have to define 'need' and that can vary tremendously. A 'modern' family, living in a three-bedroomed semi, with four children, two cats and the prospect of Granny coming to live with them might feel they badly needed more space, and most people would heartily agree! But in some parts of the world, where people live a dozen to a small hut, the 'modern' family might be thought to be living palatially.

Basically, the Universe in not mean. There is enough to go round, there is an abundance for each, for when we are uninhibited by feelings of guilt and when we are requited we become generous and accepting, and this sets up an enriching flow.

So ask for what you want, accept yourself and your needs and preferences and when your spells bear fruit give back – give back to the homeless youth who sits begging on the pavement, give back to the busker, the charity collector, the gypsy selling charms. Give to jumble sales, plant trees, sponsor environmental projects, and enjoy your giving as well as receiving, for you are part of the river of life.

For a better idea of how to go about making spells it is best also to read the companion volume in this series *Witchcraft – a beginner's guide*. This will give you information about symbols, ritual and how to form your magic circle. The two books together give you enough information to get going, but it is always best to read as widely as possible, starting with the 'Further Reading' section in both books, so you know clearly where you stand in magical matters, and that you have given the matter good thought. Remember, being well informed is important, but making up your own mind is more important still. And practice, too, is vital, or we are adrift in theory. So here goes:

PROTECTIVE CIRCLE

Visualise your protective circle as explained in Chapter 1. Say:

> 'Circle round me,
> Safe and sound, me.
> Power hold
> Till I have told.
> Blessed Be.'

When you have finished say:

> 'Circle made
> Now shall fade.
> Away, away,
> Till a new day.
> Blessed Be.'

Make sure you visualise your circle each time, and affirm that it is dispersed when your spell is finished.

To banish lovers' jealousy, resentment and strife

Do this in the bedroom. It's intended for the things that are really affecting your love, not usually for squabbles about money and kids, however irritating they may be. You can do it alone, but if your partner is involved so much the better.

Open the window. Circle slowly 'widdershins' (anticlockwise) and say:

> 'Turn and turn about,
> Out, out, out.
> Badness put to rout,
> End to every doubt
> Out, out, out'

Sweep all the hurtful, damaging emotions out of the window with your hands, imagining them as grey clouds going out and dispersing in the atmosphere.

In your oil burner place a combination of ylang-ylang, myrrh and coriander. (N.B. I always like to combine ingredients in threes and multiples thereof. This is a tradition passed down from the Celts, to whom three was a magical number. It relates to Mother, Father and Child, to the Triple Goddess and many other concepts. However, it's up to you – use other numbers if you like, when you experiment yourself.)

Now say, as you circle 'deosil' (clockwise):

> 'Winding, winding, winding,
> Peace and joy now finding
> A love that's true and binding
> Winding, winding, winding'

Replenish oil as needed.

To welcome a baby

This delightful ritual was devised by Nick and Mary Graham and printed in *Pagan Dawn* magazine. The idea, of course, is not to make any promises on behalf of the child, for she or he will make up her or his own mind when old enough. Rather the intention is to thank the gods and dedicate the child to the powers of Life.

The baby is presented to each of the elements in turn. These are Air, Fire, Earth and Water. Air is associated with East, with thought, communication, flight and swift movement; Fire with South, home of passion, heat, initiative and intuition; Water with West, direction of empathy, compassion and human insight; Earth with North, home of all that is practical, protective and sensuous. So the baby is dedicated to the elements that form us, to the powers that surround us, to the directions that define our ground and to the forces of Life itself. You might say very simply 'I dedicate this child to .....(element)', or you may like to devise something more complex.

The following are excerpts from the words used by the Grahams:

> 'Joy, health, love and peace
> Be all here in this place;
> We gather this night
> To welcome the light'

This chant can be accompanied by drumming, as all link hands to form a circle and define sacred space. At the East say: 'Let this place be filled with the joyful Dawn Chorus, with the gentle lullaby of breeze-caressed leaves, with the drowsy humming of honey bees, and the faerie song of the wind.' At the South say: 'Let this place be filled with crackling strength, with the warmth of golden, balmy days, the melody of crickets, the lazy scurrying of summer hedgerows: the scents of the noon-day sun.' At the West say: 'Let this place be filled with cool, renewing waters; the rippling brook, the sighing sea, the slap of the leaping salmon; the haunting cry of the whale; the sound of the droplet on the still pool; the peace of evening.' At the North say: 'Let this place be filled with the glittering light of the cold northern stars; with the enduring strength of the

Earth, our Mother; the tang of the heather, and the silent breath of the distant mountains.'

'We are gathered in love to give thanks to the Gods for this new life, and to present .... to the Beloved.'

'Who stands Gossip to this Little One, to cherish her and help her grow in wisdom and love? Who will nurture the seed of her promise, that she may in time unfold the full flower of her will?'

FATHER 'We, her parents, accept responsibility in all matters, for this little one, for her warmth, her shelter, her food and love.'

MOTHER 'We will take care for her being; physical, emotional and spiritual, to the utmost of our ability.'

Now the baby is given an 'inner name' for spiritual identity. Nine godparents are chosen, including the parents, two men and two women to symbolise each of the four elements and three women to embody Maiden, Mother and Crone – this applies to a girl-child. In the case of a boy the light/dark qualities of the Horned God might be represented. Please see *Witchcraft – a beginner's guide* for a more comprehensive description of Goddess and God.

Now each of the guests is invited to make a contribution of their own, perhaps in poetry or prose, and the event closes with a blessing. The Grahams chose a Quaker blessing 'in glowing celebration of babyhood'. You might say:

> 'May the Lady and the Lord bless and care for this child. May s/he grow in freedom, safety and truth. May her/his childhood be a time of joy so that s/he may take with her/him into adulthood the confidence to find her/his own true path. In the name of the Great Mother and the Horned God.'

As this is a family occasion care must be taken not to upset anyone and so words can be chosen accordingly. Last but not least, wine is shared and there is a party. This should be a ritual acceptable to all. Burning incense is hardly appropriate, especially close to a young baby. Essential oil in a burner will help to set the scene, however. Lavender is light and envigorating and ylang-ylang is sweet and gentle. However, as this occasion is important, I suggest frankincense oil, for it has majesty without being too heavy.

Money Spell

Take a green or gold candle and anoint it with oils of patchouli, geranium and orange.

Write the amount of money you need on a piece of paper. In theory, magical principles are the same whatever the amount, but if you go too high your guilt (unconscious or conscious) or disbelief may come between you and success. So opt for a reasonable amount and write it on the paper. Light your candle. Say:

> 'By heat of Sun and root of tree,
> By gleaming Moon and surge of sea,
> So ....(£, $) shall come to me'

Rub the paper also with the oils. Look at the flame for a while and imagine clearly how it will be when you get the money. Include in your imaginings some way you will benefit the Earth and fellow humans in however modest a way, when you receive the sum.

Put the paper carefully in your purse or wallet, and look after it! The money will come in a way that is quite natural, perhaps as the repayment of an outstanding debt, or an opportunity to earn more cash.

Herbal sachets or charms

These are made of herbs sewn up in squares of cloth carried as amulets or talismans, for general luck or for a specific purpose. An amulet is generally lucky, whereas a talisman is made with a specific purpose in mind. Sachets can be carried with you, for the helpful influence to remain with you at all times, or placed in a specific place, such as a drawer, or put on an altar.

When making a sachet choose material of the colour appropriate to your purpose. Here are the suggested colours:

Green Fertility, healing, love, finances and employment, general luck

Yellow   Confidence, clear thinking, study, concentration

Orange   Self-confidence, integration, making an impression, feeling 'together', attraction, stimulation

Red   Lust, energy, assertion, strength, health, protection, courage, destruction of negativity

White   Peace, truth, clarity, children

Black   Absorbing anything negative, healing serious diseases

Pink   Love, affection, friendship, reliability, kindness

Light blue   Love, peace, happiness, balance

Dark blue   Psychism, healing, the subconscious

Purple   Spirituality, healing, meditating, mental expansion

Brown   Safety, animals, the land

You can see from this list that some purposes might have more than one suitable colour, so choose the colour that feels best for you. Of course, you could make your sachet from fabric of several colours, but I think it is probably better to keep to a single colour, for concentration of energies.

Make your sachet from natural fibre such as wool, cotton or felt. It is best to cut the material into a square of at least 15 cm, or a circle of 18 cm diameter, for anything smaller may be awkward to handle – but your sachet can be larger or smaller if you wish.

Mix your chosen herbs. Empower them with your intention. Close your eyes and visualise your need. Hold your hands over the herbs, palms open, and concentrate all your energies, feeling them flowing into the herbal mixture. Open your eyes and see the herbs – imagine their natural energies increased and glowing now with the power you have put into them. Sniff them gently, and as the aroma penetrates you, know that these herbs have the power to do their job.

Place a small handful of the herbs into the middle of the cloth, lift up the edges and tie these securely with a piece of matching thread. Or you can make a more complex sachet by sewing squares or circles together, if you wish. Now breathe into the herbs, and tie the whole ritual up as you tie the thread at the top. This, like other rituals is best performed within a magic circle, with candles of the appropriate colour, incense, etc. At the very least you should visualise your protective circle around you. Don't forget to 'earth' yourself when you

have finished. Place the herbal sachet on the ground, between your hands. Place your palms flat on the floor and let any excess energy drain out into the vast body of the Earth. Now put the sachet where you want it to be and forget about it.

Love sachet

Dried rose petals, lavender and orris root. Place also a small piece of copal in the sachet – choose one that is as close to the shape of a heart as possible. Use rose-coloured material, or red for a more passionate love.

Healing a broken heart

Rose petals, cinnamon, lemon balm. Use dark blue material. Starhawk (in *The Spiral Dance*) suggests cutting a white felt heart in two and sewing it together with blue thread while you are charging the charm. Place the sewn-up heart in the charm, with the herbs.

Money sachet

Patchouli, clove and cinnamon, and three silver coins – they don't have to be real silver, 5p or 20p pieces, or dimes will do fine. Sew up in green cloth.

Success in examination

Lavender, rosemary, mace. Use yellow cloth. Draw a picture to put in the sachet, such as a stick-person, with a smiling face, perhaps wearing a mortar-board and holding a certificate.

Car protection sachet

This is given by Scott Cunningham in *Incense, Oils and Brews*: two parts rosemary, two parts juniper, one part mugwort (or wormwood), one part comfrey, one part caraway, one small quartz crystal. Tie this in red cloth and put it somewhere in the car where it won't be found. 'After a few months take the sachet apart, save and cleanse the crystal ... and use again in a new sachet.' N.B. This won't protect against careless driving!

Success sachet

Use this for interviews and any important endeavour. Place a picture representing success in the particular project in the sachet – you don't have to be artistic. Use orange cloth. Fill with lemon balm, cinnamon, ginger root. If you are naturally a confident person, and you are going for a job where thoughtfulness and practicality are likely to be prized above the more go-getting qualities, use a green sachet.

Magical baths

Immersing oneself in water is, in itself, a magical act heavy with symbolic meaning. We are all familiar with the ceremony of baptism, washing away abstract negativity in the holy waters, and however unacceptable we may find the concept of Original Sin, the cleansing properties of water, spiritually as well as physically, are undeniable.

Water is the source of all life. It covers the bulk of the planet, forms the greater part of our bodies, and life is said to have originated in the oceans. Many creation myths speak of the primordial ocean, and we all start our life floating in the waters of the womb – our self-contained amniotic universe. Cleansing and life-giving, we take water for granted, but it is a miracle, and a source of pleasure.

In *Circlework* (House of the Goddess, 1994) the priestess Shan has some unequivocal comments about the importance of the bath. She says: 'If you prefer showers, or only ever stay in a bath for five or ten minutes ... it's possible you don't permit yourself to enjoy the prolonged pleasure of warm, lazy waters because you tend to deny yourself deep, private time for inner peace. If you have another way of lying alone ... in dreaming, idle pleasure ... once or twice a week, then I'll buy it.' If not, then why not have a long, lazy bath?

So, turn your bath into a relaxing ritual. Light your bathroom with candles. Have a radio, cassette player, book, magazines – whatever you like. Take food with you – perhaps grapes and small pieces of

cheese, chocolate, pistachio nuts, anything you like to give you a feeling of self-indulgent luxury. Wine is lovely to drink while you are in the bath, but you may prefer cocoa, or any other drink. Make sure the room is warm and there are plenty of warm towels and a soft robe waiting for you when you get out. Burn incense if you wish, and ... relax.

Immersing yourself in water is therapeutic in itself, but for other, specific benefits you may like to add herbs or oils to the water. As always, clearly visualise your goal right from the start. For instance, if you wish to be rid of something – thoughts, feelings – if you have been pushed and buffeted all day, if someone has made you angry or hurt you and you can't seem to shake off the emotions, repeat to yourself, as the bath waters run 'Cleansing waters, healing waters'. Add salt or lavender oil to the water. Lower yourself slowly into the balmy waters and see all the negativity flowing out of you, dissolving and fading as the water receives it. A candle in the bathroom is beneficial, as the flame has a hypnotic effect and may serve to still the churning of your mind.

Herb baths can be made with herbal sachets, and Scott Cunningham (in *Incense, Oils and Brews*, Llewellyn, 1991) likens them to large pots of herbal tea. Herbs for the bath can be secured in cheesecloth or an old flannel or tea-towel. Herbs still on their stems could be hung under the tap, or you could just tip the herbs in as they are, except you will come out all speckled, and may risk a blocked drain. The procedure is the same as for herbal charms. You could also prepare an infusion, as described in Chapter 6, and add this to the water.

LOVE BATH

Rose, cardamom and rosemary is a suitable combination. Have your bath daily, to draw love into your life. Lie in the fragrant vapours and dream about the love that is coming to you. Visualise the sort of relationship you would like and the kind of person – but don't be too specific. Love can be found in surprising places.

Money bath

Another combination from Scott Cunningham – clove, cinnamon and galangal to warm you through and swell your finances. Relax and feel quietly confident that your finances are healthy.

To break a habit or addiction

Lemon peel, rosemary and sage. Visualise yourself clearly quite free of the habit. Let the water absorb it, neutralise it and suck it down the drain when the bath empties. Lavender or salt are also useful for this, but sage will also promote the gift of wisdom and healing.

Psychism and dreams

Thyme, bay and rose petals. This bath could be taken before bed, to encourage meaningful dreams, or before attempts at divination or scrying. Make sure you have everything organised so once you have settled in the bath you don't have to think. Let your mind drift and dissociate from the everyday. Go straight to bed, if you wish for prophetic dreams. Go smoothly into your method of divination, if that is what you have planned.

Protection

Sandalwood, bay, cinnamon. If you are undergoing a period in life where you feel attacked and threatened, or if you feel there is someone in your life who is a threat to you, take this bath daily. Visualise the waters leaving a protective film upon your body, so you are now 'thick skinned'. The herbs will give you a psychic armour that will enable you to function unimpeded and keep you safe.

PRACTICE

There is plenty in this chapter for you to practise. If you do not like the herbal combinations suggested then make up your own. Enjoy your herbs, be creative and let your imagination flow.

6

healing with herbs

O, health! health! the blessing of the rich! the riches of the poor! who can buy thee at too dear a rate, since there is no enjoying the world without thee?

Ben Jonson, *Volpone*, Act 2, Scene 1

*T*he familiar, household drugs that we turn to for colds and headaches are often herbal in origin. The active ingredient in aspirin, for instance, is salicylic acid, and this is derived from the willow tree. As a justification for the production of refined and synthetic drugs it is often said that natural sources are unreliable, varying in strength and content. This is no doubt true, and there is much in modern medicine that we would not wish to be without.

However, it is remarkable how few ailments are actually cured, despite all the technology, and many drugs have the main purpose of keeping the patient happy while Nature does its work! We forget that there may be some elements that defy scientific analysis. These we could call 'structural information' – a code passed from one living organism to another. So in consuming herbs we are taking in more than scientific formulae: we are also absorbing something of the life-essence of the plant. This applies to food as well. A juicy orange is far preferable to a vitamin C pill.

Prepared herbal remedies are readily available from many New Age centres, wholefood shops and Natural Therapy clinics. In this chapter we shall look at some simple remedies for common ailments. Here I must repeat the warning from Chapter 4 – always be very careful when diagnosing ailments yourself. Consult a qualified practitioner when there is the smallest doubt what the symptoms may mean. This is especially true in the case of children, who may worsen quickly – as they recover quickly – and who aren't always good at describing how they feel. Remember that herbs are strong. Treat them with respect. Some are not suitable for use in pregnancy, so bear this in mind.

Infusions and Decoctions

If you have grown your own herbs you will need to know how to convert them into remedies.

For an **infusion** you will need 25 g of the leaves or flowers. Place in a glass container, cover with 500 ml boiling water, leave for 10 minutes and strain. Then place the infusion in a refrigerator.

Decoction is suitable for the tougher parts of the plants such as root or bark. Using the same proportions as for an infusion simmer the herb in water for 10 minutes. Strain and refrigerate.

In each case 20 ml of the liquid is equal to 1 g of the herb, and 5 ml equals 1 teaspoon of the liquid. You can make less, or more of

course, as long as the proportions are maintained. These preparations will keep for several days in a refrigerator. They may look a strange colour, but that doesn't matter. Use herbs that you have freshly picked from your window box or garden, and as you gather them think about what you are going to use them for. You may like to repeat a phrase softly to yourself, for example: 'Sage, sage, heal a sore throat'.

ᎬᎷᏢᎾᎳᎬᎡᏆᎡᎶ ᎽᎾᎢᎡ ᎡᎬᎷᎬᎠᏏᎬᏚ

To align your own healing energies with those of the herb you may like to perform a short ritual. Create your protective circle and light a green candle. Perhaps burn an incense of rosemary, juniper and lemon balm, or your preferred blend. Sit in the centre of your circle, cross-legged, or however is most comfortable for you, facing north. (North is associated with the element Earth. In the northern hemisphere this is the dark part of the sky where we never see the fiery Sun. Readers in the southern hemisphere may prefer to face south, as the associations are usually reversed.) Hold the brew in your lap, between your palms.

If you are familiar with opening your chakras, do so now. Circulate the energies as described under 'Healing energies' in Chapter 4. When you are ready, direct the energy into the potion, imagining the person you are healing completely well – this is more effective than to imagine the ailment improving, because any visualisation of the complaint itself can direct some of the energy the wrong way. Repeat: '......... (name) is completely well. In the name of the Great Mother. So may it be.'

If you cannot open your chakras then you may simply imagine your own healing energies entering the potion from your pressed palms. Make a final offering of incense, give thanks and close down your chakras and your circle thoroughly. Your potion of healing herbs, strengthened by your own intention, is now ready for use.

Remedies for common ailments

Notes on dosage   All dosages are recommended for adults. Dosages need to be reduced for children, starting with one-quarter dose at age 4 and rising to full dose at about age 15, depending to some extent on the size of the child – but remember, a large child still only has a metabolism which corresponds to his or her age.

Back pain and sciatica

Lavender oil will relax tautened muscles and give a feeling of warmth. Sciatica is especially nasty, and feels, as one sufferer described, as if someone has pulled a string up the back of your leg. Sciatica originates from a pressed nerve in the spine. Massage wherever the patient wishes, as to induce relaxation is the best remedy you can provide. Be careful when massaging the spine, however. If there is a slipped disc you could make matters much worse.

Constipation

A common modern malady where there isn't enough fibre in the diet. However, fibre isn't the only factor, and it is possible to have too much fibre, believe it or not, especially for children who may be better eating white bread, which gives their digestive systems time to absorb the nutrients. Constipation can be caused by tension – the teeth-gritting kind, which will have a corresponding rigidifying action on the bowel. The bowel readily responds to emotional states, and constipation is as frequent a reaction as diarrhoea.

For constipation it is important that there is enough fluid in the diet – as much as four litres a day. Valerian is good for anxious constipation. It is ruled by Mercury, hence its 'mobile' quality! Take two to twelve teaspoons of the infusion three times a day.

Cystitis

This painful, nagging complaint is the bane of many women. The best treatment for cystitis is to go to bed with a large jug of water or very weak squash, and to make sure you drink a glass every half hour. A hot water bottle on the abdomen eases acute attacks. An acupuncturist friend suggests drinking several litres of water and then having a single cup of fairly strong coffee (apart from this, coffee, strong tea and alcohol should be avoided, as they irritate the bladder). Then continue drinking water. This remedy may help to flush the condition out of the system.

Marion Green in *The Magical Lore of Herbs* recommends couchgrass for cystitis. She says that a decoction of the roots of this plant (which are maddeningly persistent to gardeners) made her feel better within a day and cleared the complaint in a week, and that is as good as any antibiotic. The botanical name for couchgrass is *Agropyron repens*, in case the common name is unfamiliar in some regions. It is also called twitch, or witchgrass, and is ruled by Jupiter, as the expansive nature of the roots might indicate!

Diarrhoea

Thyme, ruled by Venus, is good for soothing churning bowel upsets and infections. Take two to twelve teaspoons three times a day.

Feverish colds and 'flu

This is a virtually never-fail remedy for the sort of achy cold that you feel coming on in advance. You will need organic lemons and preferably organic, locally made honey. Place a tablespoon of honey in a thick glass and half-fill with boiling water. This dissolves the honey. Then add the squeezed juice of one lemon and top up generously with whisky! Take this early in the evening and again before going to bed. Its effects can be quite amazing. Lemons are rich in vitamin C and ruled by the healing energies of the Moon, but this recipe owes a lot to the warmth of the whisky, I think! Even quite small children can be given a little whisky on occasion.

Strictly speaking, however, it is illegal in Britain to give alcohol to the very young, even in their own home.

Garlic is also good for colds, catarrh and bronchitis and taking it daily can improve resistance. Garlic is ruled by Mars. It is warm and expunging and was used against the plague. The best way to take garlic is raw, one to two cloves per day, but that may be rather antisocial, so one perle three times a day may be kinder to your friends!

Headache

We have already seen, in Chapter 4, that lavender can be very effective for headache. Rosemary infusion is also good – take two to eight teaspoons three times a day. Ruled by the Sun, rosemary is invigorating for headaches caused by tension or depression. For migraine, feverfew – ruled by soothing Venus – is good, and this is believed to apply to both the green and golden feverfew leaves. For this a fresh leaf can be eaten three times a day. Some people put the leaves in sandwiches, but if your symptoms include vomiting you are doing quite well even to swallow the leaf, so this is not necessarily a remedy to apply at the time of an attack. It is best to take feverfew regularly to prevent or reduce attacks. Avoid feverfew in pregnancy.

Insomnia

Usually there is no medical reason whatsoever for sleeplessness, for it is the body's natural reaction to sleep when it is sleepy. However, when worry and tension build up it is not always so easy to sleep, and it is then a very short step to worry about not sleeping and entering a neurotic vicious circle. Naturally sedatives are best avoided. For insomnia, especially where there are muscular aches, a massage with lavender oil is very soothing. You can massage yourself or better still get someone else to do it. Dilute oil in carrier, as discussed in Chapter 4, two drops per teaspoon. Lavender oil placed in a burner can also help, and the dancing flame of the nightlight can be hypnotic.

Rheumatism, aches and pains, cramp

All these respond to the loosening, relaxing effect of lavender.

Sore throat and tonsilitis

This is treatable by sage infusion, which I have found to be very good. Hearty sage is a Jupiter herb. Children also like a teaspoon of honey when they have sore throats, and it can make the infusion go down better. The dosage is two to six teaspoons three times a day for adults, and it is best used as a gargle. Young children may find this difficult, however. Do not take sage internally during pregnancy.

Menstruation

Menstruation is certainly not an illness. In general it is our attitudes to it that need to be healed. It is a great shame to refer to periods as 'the curse' for in that way the rhythms of femininity are being cursed. In some respects the pervasive attitude of patriarchy is to regard the Feminine with suspicion, at best. This needs to be changed, so that the special experience and power of the monthly rhythm can be respected for the important cultural force that it is. Accomplishing this would, I am sure, go a long way towards dispelling most of what we call 'PMT' or 'PMS'.

The best place to start is with attitude. If your periods give you problems start by respecting them. If you do not feel like doing certain things at certain times of the month then, as far as possible, don't do them. Many tribal societies are documented as isolating women at the time of their periods, and this has been interpreted as the women being 'unclean'. It is much more likely that women were put to one side because they were especially powerful and perhaps needed time to meditate and dream in order to bring their special contribution to tribal life. Most women would approach isolation during the period with great glee. Imagine the peace! Give yourself as much peace as you possibly can, if you feel you need it.

In a culture that values transcendence and devalues immanence (or a sense of 'indwelling' deity) the opportunity for mystical participation in the natural world, the world of the body, that is offered by the period is ignored, or treated with contempt or disbelief. The period is a time of openness, of truth and may offer opportunities for shamanic experience. Women may feel especially vulnerable now, but in a safe environment the full possibilities of this time can be explored. Burn an incense of dragon's blood, wormwood and frankincense to encourage psychic powers and protection.

Press some violets in a circular frame and use them as a focus in meditation. Violets were said to have sprung from the blood of the dying god Attis. Attis is one of the many dying and resurrecting gods, and so the violet is a symbol of transformation and regeneration, which is what happens at the period. The planetary ruler of the violet is Venus, and their enchanting, thoughtful little 'faces' are calming, and speak of the mute sentience of the plant kingdom.

Jane Brideson, who illustrated this book, recommends the essential oil clary sage to ease congestion and discomfort prior to the period. You can use it in the bath, rub it on yourself, or better still get a partner to rub your back. Clary sage is ruled by the Moon, and of course the lunar cycle is closely linked to the menstrual rhythm. Clary sage is heady and woody, good as a tonic for the nerves and as a mild sedative. It is a strong herb and should certainly be avoided in pregnancy until the latter stages as it may encourage uterine contractions. Clary sage can be reserved for this special time as a way of marking and honouring it. In addition, valerian, chamomile and peppermint are all helpful for relieving period pains.

Although periods are a female experience, men needn't be excluded. A man can learn much from his partner's menstrual cycle in terms of sensitivity and responsiveness. Also the monthly rhythm can put him in touch with his own cyclicity. Activities of the couple or family may be modulated according to the menstrual cycle, which is likely to have a relationship to the lunar cycle. Such rhythms are soothing, and help to give a structure and basis to life, which is one of the functions of the Feminine principle in society.

Pregnancy

Pregnancy is a condition that can bring many discomforts, culminating in the supreme event of labour.

Probably the most useful thing you can do for yourself during pregnancy is learn to relax, know your own body and be honest with yourself. Oil burners and massage are a wonderful aid to relaxation as we have seen. Lavender and ylang-ylang are especially pleasant to use. There are many helpful books on pregnancy and childbirth, explaining the process and giving advice for management of labour – Sheila Kitzinger is a well-known and recommended writer on this subject – and ante-natal classes are available to all.

It is widely accepted that one medical intervention in the birth process leads on to another, and so it is by far the best to have as natural a birth as possible. Although medical professionals are not always supportive of home births, these seem generally to be the safest and easiest for mother and child, because the pregnant woman naturally feels more relaxed in her own home.

Oils and massage can be a great help during labour, but please be realistic. If you are the sort of person who gets hysterical at a visit to the dentist, oils and the sound of a drumbeat coming from a cassette player are going to be fairly useless. Birth is indescribably painful for most women – not all, but most. The contractions suck you down into a deep, dark cave, where you feel at one with the primal forces, the Mother Goddess herself – and you are aware that this isn't all sugary, sentimental and beautiful by any means! You probably won't want to talk – in fact you may not be able to, for you may revert to an instinctual, pre-verbal state, and all that exists in the whole Universe is the pain and power of what you are going through.

Tension is an enemy during the birth process as it inhibits the effectiveness of contractions and makes pain worse. You may want to move around, you may opt for a water-birth. Give a great deal of thought to what may be right for you and keep your options open. You may wish to choose a blend of essential oils for your birth-partner to rub on your back or belly. My choice for my third child

was a combination of geranium, lavender and orange. I thought this would be soothing, invigorating and encouraging, and it did smell nice, in fact. However, in the event I went into strong labour very quickly and the oils were about as much use as a woolly hat in an earthquake! I do not say any of this to create fear, for pain is certainly not the same as horror, and the pain of birth is a unique experience, productive as it is. However, I have known first-time mums make difficulties for themselves through believing it could all be made easy, and then, shocked by the actuality of the experience, making things worse for themselves than they need have been. For the lucky few things may be easy, but it is best to be realistic.

Raspberry leaf is reputed to be good for safe birth and raspberry tea is quite pleasant. It can be taken in gradually increasing doses during the last two months of pregnancy to increase the efficiency of uterine contractions.

Aromatherapy for Pregnancy and Childbirth by Margaret Fawcett gives some helpful hints on care during pregnancy, labour and after birth – details of this book are given in the 'Further Reading' section. The use of herbs and aromatherapy in pregnancy is a subject in itself. I have touched on it here because it is such a feminine experience, and witchcraft, herbal lore and lunar lore are all part of the body of knowledge that we may call 'feminine'. They are just as available to men, however, for although men cannot have first-hand experience of pregnancy, it is important to them to be able to develop their instinctual side also.

OILS AND HERBS TO AVOID IN PREGNANCY

Here is a list of oils that should be avoided in pregnancy: aniseed, armoise, arnica (not the same as the homeopathic remedy), basil, camphor, carraway, cinnamon, clove, cedarwood, fennel, hyssop, marjoram, mugwort, myrrh, nutmeg, origanum, pennyroyal, sage, savory, tansy, tarragon, thuja, thyme, wintergreen. Also be very cautious with chamomile, clary sage, peppermint, rose, rosemary.

Herbs to avoid are feverfew and sage. Naturally this is not intended to be an exhaustive list. I have commented on the herbs covered here, but always approach anything unfamiliar with great caution in pregnancy.

A pregnancy meditation

Place an oil that you like in your burner – ylang-ylang or lavender may be good choices. Turn off all the lights; the glow of the nightlight in the burner should be sufficient. Relax deeply, as described in Chapter 1 and visualise.

You are out walking on a moonlit night. Walk slowly. Notice the feel of the air, the fragrances, the way the landscape looks, shimmering in the pale light. Take some time over this, see the beauty of the white Moon, like a great, round egg. Absorb the peace....

[*Short pause*]

You find yourself at the top of a slope. Below you there stretches a lake, shining in the moonlight. The Full Moon is ahead of you, casting a silver path upon the water. There is a small boat on the water lapping against the shores of the lake....

[*Short pause*]

Walk slowly down to the boat and get in. There are soft cushions on the bottom of the boat. Lie down and make yourself comfortable. Know that this boat is safe and strong, and will hold you securely on the journey that you are about to take. Do you wish to take it? If so, the boat now gently begins to drift out into the middle of the moonlit lake, rocking gently from side to side....

[*Short pause*]

The boat now drifts into a cave. The moonlight is lost. All is dark. Around you there is a smell of the very depths of the Earth, sweet, damp and mysterious. In this cave you are to meet something or someone that will prepare you for the experience of motherhood. Just take time for any images, feelings, memories to come to the surface.

[*Do not be frightened. Whatever you see or experience is intended to be helpful, and if it seems alarming at first that is because it has not been understood. Five minutes pause.*]

Now your boat drifts out into the moonlight again. Slowly, gently you move over the pearly lake, until your boat comes to rest on the other side. When you are ready, get out of the boat and walk up the slope into this new landscape. Feel changed and renewed. Come back to everyday awareness when you are ready.

You may like to record this on to a tape, so that you can relax properly while visualising. Write your experiences in a notebook. Make sure you have a friend to talk over anything that may come to your mind, if you are the sort of person who may be easily disturbed. You may prefer to alter the central section 'In this cave you are to meet something or someone...' to a suggestion about talking to your unborn baby, instead, getting to know her or him in this waiting time.

pRACTICe

You will have an opportunity to practise your healing skills when you, a member of your family or a friend are sick. Massage, of course, can be practised at any time. You can't really go wrong with infusions and decoctions, so it is a shame to use up a plant when you don't need to.

You may like to build up your stock of oils further, or acquire new plants if you are growing your own. Don't forget to note any impressions or thoughts in your special notebook.

COOKING
MAGICALLY

*...And when you crush an apple with your teeth,
say to it in your heart:*

'Your seeds shall live in my body,

*And the buds of your tomorrow shall blossom in
my heart'...*

Kahlil Gibran, *The Prophet*

*C*ooking magically is like doing anything else magically. It means
participating fully in what you are doing, it means appreciating
the importance of it and being alive to its many meanings and
implications – and it means enjoying it.

In daily life cooking magically may be hard to keep up. You may be shattered after a long day at work, the kids may be clamouring or you may be in a hurry to go out. In ancient times humans were probably more aware of the Divine in day-to-day life, and when one sees women from other cultures gracefully (and apparently happily) going through their chores the vestiges of this seem to linger. Attempting to recreate this in totality, immediately, may be making too great a demand on ourselves, however. So if you let it slip for a while you can pick it up again, when you can, without guilt.

Preparing food 'magically' requires the following conditions, in my opinion:

1 Use ingredients that are as far as possible natural. Use tins and packets only with care, after carefully reading the label for the contents.

2 Use ingredients that have been produced in a thoughtful way – organic vegetables, home-grown produce when possible. If you are a meat-eater, try to obtain meat that has been reared in kindly conditions, fed with natural ingredients and killed humanely. Look for 'free-range' pork and poultry, and avoid veal. Always use free-range eggs.

3 Use herbs creatively – so much the better if you have grown them yourself.

4 Don't cook when you are tired, crotchety, anxious or tense with PMS. Either get someone else to do it or eat simply. Bread, cheese and fruit is a balanced meal, baked beans on wholemeal toast is packed with protein.

5 Enjoy cooking. If you really hate the whole business keep things simple or pass the job to someone else – teenagers are often creative about cooking, although not so good about the washing-up! If you cook under duress, your resentment will infiltrate the food in a subtle way – or not so subtle, for unconsciously you may sabotage your efforts, overdoing the salt or garlic. In addition, you are likely to get small burns and scalds and to feel hot and bothered.

If all this seems impossible, just consider. Macaroni cheese, served with organic tomatoes and garnished with fresh parsley from your

window box, an omelette of free-range eggs flavoured with a little marjoram or oregano, free-range pork sausages served with organic potatoes, boiled with fresh mint leaves and another vegetable as available – all these are simple meals, quite quick to prepare. So if you are busy, don't despair. You can still cook with natural ingredients, even if, like most of us, you do resort to packets at times.

There is a lot of debate about whether we should or should not eat meat. Whatever choice is made, one thing is certain – life depends on death and is perpetuated by death. There is no getting away from this. The attempts of humans to come to terms with this are evident even in Stone Age art, where the wish of the hunter to achieve success in the hunt and still preserve the essential unity of creation are suggested and depicted in many ways. If we choose not to eat meat, we still have to kill to live, for while we may think it is more noble to kill a cabbage, we are still depriving the cabbage of life, when all is said and done.

It is interesting how one can know things and yet somehow not fully appreciate them. This interdependence of life and death became a vivid reality for me in one unforgettable moment some years ago. It was an ordinary family scene, in the kitchen, and my middle son was tucking into a salad, which included beans I had sprouted myself. There sat this healthy, cheery child, shovelling beansprouts into his mouth. They quivered on his lips, crunched between his teeth, and disappeared inexorably down his throat in between intermittent chatter about his day. Those things were alive! Have you heard the phrase 'screaming from the garden'? Well, these sprouts were screaming from my draining board, where, only moments before they were enjoying their vitality. I could feel their death-pangs. What was life, enjoyment, health to us was death to them, and for a moment the dinner table looked like a battlefield.

Of course, I am not saying one should be sentimental about a beansprout, but living magically involves, I believe, an appreciation of these things. You may like to mark this by saying a simple grace, such as 'Thank you for giving your lives, to feed ours', as suggested by the priestess, Shan. Perhaps you could say 'Thanks to the Goddess, for providing us with delicious food' or 'Blessings upon the

Earth and all that has given itself to go into this meal'. If there are sceptics or mocking teenagers at your table, you may prefer to say these things silently. But we need to remember what gives us life if we are to know our place in the scheme of things, and herbs certainly give their lives to feed ours.

Recipes

There are many excellent recipe books available, all making full use of herbs and spices. The following recipes are chosen for their simplicity.

Chinese Chicken

This was suggested to me by an acupuncturist friend who knows about Chinese medicine. He recommends it especially when there may be a feeling of 'cold' in the stomach, following a 'bug' or bout of diarrhoea.

For each person you will need one piece of free-range chicken and one carrot. Chop the carrot into slivers and add a mixture of stir-fry vegetables to taste. Cook the chicken in the oven. When it is just about cooked, stir fry the vegetables, including a piece of chopped root ginger. The size of the piece of ginger really depends on your taste, but the more the merrier, within reason (ginger is ruled by Mars and is warming). Skin and chop the ginger into small pieces before adding it to the pan – some people prefer to soak it first. Add fresh garlic to taste (Mars again). Cut up the chicken and add it to the mixture – don't use chicken that has been cooled for it can be dangerous to reheat meat. Serve the dish with boiled rice and *shoyu* (soy sauce made from naturally fermented soya beans) – delicious!

Vegetarian Spaghetti Sauce

This is for four people. You will need 225 g (8 oz) green lentils. I find these are meatier than the red split lentils, and less prone to have

small stones with them. Rinse the lentils and simmer them for about three-quarters of an hour or until soft. If you soak the lentils first, they will take less time to cook. These green lentils are also called continental lentils.

Finely chop a large onion and fry this along with fresh garlic. You may add other vegetables such as grated carrot, mushrooms, capsicums or courgettes. When the onion is transparent, add a tin of tomatoes, or use six fresh tomatoes, skinned by first being covered with boiling water. Add two tablespoons of tomato puree, salt to taste, freshly ground pepper and fresh herbs, such as parsley and oregano/ marjoram – one tablespoon of each chopped fresh herb. Add the cooked, drained lentils and a good spoonful of Marmite. Add hot water as required, simmer for ten minutes, taste and adjust seasoning.

You can serve this with spaghetti – it's especially tasty with grated cheese on the top – or use it to replace the meat sauce in lasagne. If you are using it in lasagne, reserve some of the tomato juice, as the mixture may be too runny otherwise.

SPROUTING BEANS

This is really easy and freshly sprouted beans are rich in vitamin C. You can eat them raw or stir fry.

Any beans can be sprouted as long as they aren't split peas or lentils. The best beans are the little green beans called mung beans. Beans increase hugely in size as they sprout, so start with about three tablespoons. Wash them and leave them to soak overnight in water. The next day rinse them in cold, running water and place them in a jar. Cover the top of the jar with a clean piece of old tea-towel, secured by an elastic band. Now keep the beans in a warm, fairly dark place, rinsing and draining about three times a day to remove toxins. Keep the jar in a dark cupboard: the sprouts are whiter if kept dark. You could cover the jar with a towel or brown paper. When the beans are sprouted they are ready for use, either eaten raw in a salad or sandwich, or cooked in a favourite recipe.

YOGURT BOWL COOLER

This is a refreshing accompaniment to Indian meals, given by Evelyn Findlater in her *Wholefood Cookery Course*. It is a lovely way to use fresh mint, which is so easy to grow. Incidentally, it's really easy to make your own yogurt. Mix one pint of sterilised milk with two tablespoons of skimmed milk powder and one carton of live natural yogurt, without additives. Keep this at blood heat, in an airing cupboard or yogurt-maker for four to six hours, until it has 'yogged'. Alternatively, you can use ordinary milk, boiled and simmered for 10 minutes and cooled to touchable temperature before mixing.

For the 'cooler' you will need 275 ml (½ pint) live natural yogurt, 225 g (8 oz) diced cucumber, one level teaspoon (5 ml) clear honey, one tablespoon (15 ml) chopped fresh mint, salt and freshly ground black pepper, half a teaspoon (2.5 ml) paprika and one teaspoon (5 ml) chopped fresh mint to garnish.

Mix all this together and sprinkle on the paprika and chopped mint. This is lovely with a hot curry.

PRACTICE

If you want to cook 'magically' then get organised. Sit down for a moment and think about alterations you may need to make in your routine. Don't be too ambitious. Make lists of simple menus and shopping you will need to do. It may be better to cook several meals at weekends or while you are in the mood, and keep them in fridge or freezer until needed. Don't make too many new demands on yourself at once – take things slowly and have fun with your ingredients.

Useful address   The Soil Association, 86 Colston Street, Bristol BS1 5BB, England. Tel: 01179 290661. Promotes organic farming and protecting the environment – lists and information for which there may be a small charge.

APPENDIX 1
HERBS AND YOUR SUN SIGN

We have looked repeatedly at the links between herbs and astrology. It is possible to use the energies in herbs to enhance the qualities of your Sun sign, whether as incense, essential oils, herbal baths or sachets. Here is a quick guide to herbs that are suitable. Of course, to know more about your entire astrological make-up you need your birth chart drawn up. This could give you valuable information – for instance, maybe you have many planets in a sign other than your Sun sign, and this will affect you greatly. For now, however, we must stay with Sun sign alone.

Aries   Mars herbs will intensify your fire and verve. Sun herbs are also good. Cedar, cinnamon, copal, dragon's blood.

Taurus   Venus herbs will harmonise with your love of comfort. Saturn herbs, for example patchouli, match your practical nature. Cardamom, patchouli, rose, thyme.

Gemini   Mercury herbs match your versatility and mental agility. Venus herbs could help creativity and just a pinch of Saturn for concentration. Lavender, mace, parsley, peppermint.

Cancer   Moon herbs, for your emotional nature, and sometimes a little Jupiter to brighten you up. Calamus, eucalyptus, lemon balm, myrrh.

Leo   Sun herbs for lordly Leo, also sometimes Jupiter. Benzoin, frankincense, juniper, rosemary.

Virgo   Mercury herbs, sometimes Saturn for these self-possessed lovers of detail. Cypress, fennel, lavender, patchouli.

Libra   Venus herbs for harmonious Libra. A little Mercury for clear thought. Rose, spearmint, thyme, violet.

Scorpio   Choose from Mars and Moon herbs for the strong nature and feelings of Scorpio. Basil, ginger, myrrh, violet.

Sagittarius   Jupiter herbs for ebullient Sagittarius. Also sometimes Sun herbs. Clove, copal, frankincense, sage.

Capricorn   Saturn herbs for controlled and practical Capricorn. A little Venusian influence could lighten things up. Cypress, patchouli, comfrey, vervain.

Aquarius   Saturn again, but also Mercury for detached Aquarians. Benzoin, cypress, lavender, pine.

Pisces   Jupiter and Moon (sometimes Venus) for this dreamy sign. Calamus, eucalyptus, sage, ylang-ylang.

In addition we can use herbs to balance our nature, and although we might not find such herbs so congenial, if they are cleverly blended with our compatible herbs they could help us to find more concealed elements in our nature. So, **Aries** might like to experiment with Moon and Venus herbs; **Taurus** with Sun, Mars and Mercury; **Gemini** with Moon and Jupiter; **Cancer** with Sun and Mars; **Leo** with Moon and Saturn; **Virgo** with Sun and Jupiter; **Libra** with Mars and Sun; **Scorpio** with Jupiter and Mercury; **Sagittarius** with Moon and Saturn; **Aquarius** with Moon and Sun; **Pisces** with Mercury, Sun and Mars.

Of course, the lore about a specific herb might encourage you to associate it with a sign. For instance, elder is ruled by Venus. However, it has a sinister and uncanny reputation. Witches were said to turn themselves into elder trees as a disguise, and spirits inhabit the branches. Judas was said to have hung himself from an elder tree. These stories might suggest the mysterious aura of Scorpio or the sometime 'weirdness' of Pisces rather than Venus-ruled Taurus or Libra. Surprisingly, I have seen elder linked with Aquarius. So there are lots of ideas to play with.

APPENDIX 2
THE WHEEL OF THE YEAR

The Wheel of the Year is the cycle of the seasons. There are many meanings attached to this – mythological, symbolic, psychological – and observing the Wheel is certainly a way of feeling in tune with the natural world, and with our own rhythms.

Traditionally there are eight festivals in the Wheel. These are:

Samhain (Hallowe'en) 31 October
Yule (Winter Solstice/Christmas) 22 December
Imbolc (Candlemas) 2 February
Spring Equinox 21 March
Beltane (May Eve) 30 April
Midsummer (Summer Solstice) 22 June
Lammas (Lughnasadh) 31 July
Autumn Equinox 21 September

These festivals celebrate the changing face of the Mother Goddess – sometimes Maiden, sometimes Mother and sometimes Wise Crone – and the dying and resurrecting God, Her son/lover, who is the personification of Nature. There is much poetry and beauty – not to mention considerable history – in this tradition. Observing it leads to inner and outer harmony. Herbs may play a considerable part in this, as seasonal incenses and in other ways. We are all familiar with the fact that holly and mistletoe are linked to Yule for instance, and there are many associations, either established or associations we can develop, between specific plants and other festivals.

This is an important subject in itself, for plants are the most obvious manifestation of changing seasons. I have listed some plants associated with each festival, together with an appropriate incense

blend. *The Wheel of the Year – a beginner's guide* in this series, covers seasonal associations much more comprehensively.

Samhain   Apples, nuts. Incense: frankincense, galangal, myrrh

Yule   Holly, ivy, mistletoe. Incense: frankincense, sandalwood, orange peel, juniper, rosemary, clove

Imbolc   Snowdrops. Incense: frankincense, calamus, rose petals

Spring Equinox   Primroses, daffodils. Incense: frankincense, benzoin, orange peel, sandalwood, nutmeg, rose petals

Beltane   Hawthorn, elder. Incense: copal, frankincense, cardamom, rose petals, orange peel, patchouli

Midsummer   Summer flowers. Incense: rose petals, sandalwood, copal, thyme, rosemary and vervain with a few drops of red wine

Lammas/Lughnasadh   Poppies, wheat. Incense: frankincense, juniper, sandalwood with a little myrrh, possibly

Autumn Equinox   Hedgerow fruits, apples, wheat. Incense: sandalwood, juniper, cypress

USEFUL INFORMATION

FURTHER READING

Witchcraft – a beginner's guide, Teresa Moorey, Hodder & Stoughton, 1996. Helpful as an introduction to witchcraft. Also read some of the books recommended in the 'Further Reading' section of the book if you wish to know more about magic and the ancient craft of the wise.

The Complete Book of Herbs, Lesley Bremness, Dorling Kindersley, 1993. A scrumptious, glossy 'coffee-table' book, beautifully illustrated, full of history, lore and loads of practical information.

Teach Yourself Herbs, Susie White, Hodder & Stoughton, 1993. A very useful book – comprehensive, clear and interesting.

The Magical Lore of Herbs, Marion Davies, Capall Bann, 1994. One of many good books from this author, this is a 'must' for herbal lore.

Encyclopedia of Magical Herbs, Scott Cunningham, Llewellyn, 1994; *The Complete Book of Incense, Oils and Brews*, same author and publisher, 1991. These really are invaluable for magical know-how, information on brews and incense recipes. The Encyclopedia has lots of herbal lore.

The Enchanted Forest, Yvonne Aburrow, Capall Bann, 1993. Trees are 'herbs' too, and this book is full of fascinating information.

Culpeper's Complete Herbal, Nicholas Culpeper, Foulsham. Culpeper was an astrologer-physician who lived in the seventeenth century. It's good to have this on your shelf for reference.

A Guide to Herbal Remedies, Mark Evans MNIMH, C. W. Daniel, 1990. Useful and clear about herbal remedies.

Aromatherapy for You at Home, Franzesca Watson, Natural by Nature Oils, 1991. Informative booklet about the basics of oils.

The Aromatherapy Handbook, Daniele Ryman, C. W. Daniel, 1990. Interesting and clearly written by someone who obviously loves and knows her subject.

Aromatherapy for Pregnancy and Childbirth, Margaret Fawcett RGN RM LLSA, Element, 1993. A very soothing and helpful book, giving a natural approach to this special time.

Suppliers

Magic and ritual

The Sorcerer's Apprentice   Mail order business operating throughout the world. Full range of incense ingredients, prepared incense, essential oils, books and occult equipment. 6–8 Burley Lodge Road, Leeds LS6 1QP, UK. Tel: 0113 245 1309. Send two first class stamps (or International Reply Coupons) for complete list.

Starchild   Mail order worldwide and shop. Incense ingredients, prepared incense, essential oils, books, candles and other products. The Courtyard, 2–4 High Street, Glastonbury, Somerset BA6 9DU, UK. Tel: 01458 834663. Send £1.50 for catalogue, which includes useful information on herbs – magical, medical, seasonal and astrological, plus recipes.

Enchantments   Worldwide mail order. Catalogue $3.00 USA, $5.00 elsewhere (US money orders only please). Herbs, incense, books (over 2,000 titles) jewellery, crystals, essential oils, candles, tarot readings, magical apothecary, crystal balls and more.

'The Goddess is alive and living in Enchantments' Open seven days a week. 341 East 9th Street (Between 1st and 2nd Avenue) New York City, NY 10003, USA. Tel: 212 228 4394.

The Eye of the Cat Worldwide mail order. Herb catalogue
$10.00; Hermetic Catalogue $10.00. 500 c refundable on first order.
Herbs, candles, incense, root, statues, posters, tarot cards, essential
oils, jewellery and books, exotic herbs and hermetic supplies. Open
seven days a week. 3314 E. Broadway, Long Beach, CA 90803, USA.
Tel: 310 438 3569.

Mysterys Mail order supplier of herbs and essential oils for magic
and ritual. 386 Darling Street, Balmain, NSW 2041, Australia.

Herbal Remedies

United Kingdom

Culpeper
Hadstock Road
Linton
Cambridge
CB1 6NJ
Tel: 01223 891196

Phyto Products Ltd
Park Works
Park Road
Mansfield Woodhouse
Notts
NG19 8EF
Tel: 01623 644334

Potter's Herbal Supplies Ltd
Leyland Mill Lane
Wigan
Lancs
WN1 2SB
Tel: 01942 234761

United States

Potter's Herbal Supplies
Regent Bond Ltd
159 West 53rd Street
Suite 35H
New York
NY 10019

All the above have a mail-order service.

Other titles in this series

Chakras   The body's energy centres, the chakras, can act as gateways to healing and increased self-knowledge. This book shows you how to work with chakras in safety and with confidence.

Chinese Horoscopes   In the Chinese system of horoscopes, the *year* of birth is all-important. *Chinese Horoscopes for beginners* tells you how to determine your own Chinese horoscope, what personality traits you are likely to have, and how your fortunes may fluctuate in years to come.

Dowsing   People all over the world have used dowsing since the earliest times. This book shows how to start dowsing – what to use, what to dowse, and what to expect when subtle energies are detected.

Dream Interpretation   This fascinating introduction to the art and science of dream interpretation explains how to unravel the meaning behind dream images to interpret your own and other people's dreams.

Feng Shui   This beginner's guide to the ancient art of luck management will show you how to increase your good fortune and well-being by harmonising your environment with the natural energies of the earth.

Gems and Crystals   For centuries gems and crystals have been used as an aid to healing and meditation. This guide tells you all you need to know about choosing, keeping and using stones to increase your personal awareness and improve your well-being.

Graphology   Graphology, the science of interpreting handwriting to reveal personality, is now widely accepted and used throughout the world. This introduction will enable you to make a comprehensive analysis of your own and other people's handwriting to reveal the hidden self.

I Ching   The roots of *I Ching* or the *Book of Changes* lie in the time of the feudal mandarin lords of China, but its traditional wisdom is still relevant today. Using the original poetry in its translated form, this introduction traces its history, survival and modern-day applications.

Love Signs   This is a practical introduction to the astrology of romantic relationships. It explains the different roles played by each of the planets, focusing particularly on the position of the Moon at the time of birth.

Meditation   This beginner's guide gives simple, clear instructions to enable you to start meditating and benefiting from this ancient mental discipline immediately. The text is illustrated throughout by full-colour photographs and line drawings.

Numerology   Despite being scientifically based, numerology requires no great mathematical talents to understand. This introduction gives you all the information you will need to understand the significance of numbers in your everyday life.

Paganism   Pagans are true Nature worshippers who celebrate the cycles of life. This guide describes pagan festivals and rituals and takes a detailed look at the many forms of paganism practised today.

Palmistry   Palmistry is the oldest form of character reading still in use. This illustrated guide shows you exactly what to look for and how to interpret what you find.

Runes   The power of the runes in healing and giving advice about relationships and life in general has been acknowledged since the time of the Vikings. This book shows how runes can be used in our technological age to increase personal awareness and stimulate individual growth.

Star Signs   This detailed analysis looks at each of the star signs in turn and reveals how your star sign affects everything about you. This book shows you how to use this knowledge in your relationships and in everyday life.

Tarot   Tarot cards have been used for many centuries. This guide gives advice on which sort to buy, where to get them and how to use them. The emphasis is on using the cards positively, as a tool for gaining self-knowledge, while exploring present and future possibilities.

The Moon and You   The phase of the Moon when you were born radically affects your personality. This book looks at nine lunar types – how they live, love, work and play, and provides simple tables to find out the phase of your birth.

Visualisation   This introduction to visualisation, a form a self-hypnosis widely used by Buddhists, will show you how to practise the basic techniques – to relieve stress, improve your health and increase your sense of personal well-being.

Witchcraft   This guide to the ancient religion based on Nature worship answers many of the questions and uncovers the myths and misconceptions surrounding witchcraft. Mystical rituals and magic are explained and there is advice for the beginner on how to celebrate the sabbats.

To order this series

All books in this series are available from bookshops or, in case of difficulty, can be ordered direct from the publisher. Just fill in the form below. Prices and availability subject to change without notice.

Buy four books from the selection below and get free postage and packaging. Just send a cheque or postal order made payable to *Bookpoint Limited* to the value of the total cover price of four books. This should be sent to: Hodder & Stoughton *Educational*, 39 Milton Park, Abingdon, Oxon OX14 4TD, UK. EMail address: orders@bookpoint.co.uk. Alternatively, if you wish to buy fewer than four books, the following postage and packaging costs apply:

UK & BFPO: £4.30 for the one book; £6.30 for two books; £8.30 for three books. Overseas and Eire: £4.80 for one book; £7.10 for 2 or 3 books (surface mail).

If you would like to pay by credit card, our centre team would be delighted to take your order by telephone. Our direct line (44) 01235 400414 (lines open 9.00 am–6.00 pm, Monday to Saturday, with a 24 hour answering service). Alternatively you can send a fax to (44) 01235 400454.

Please send me

	copies of 0 340 62082 X	Chakras		£5.99	£
	copies of 0 340 64804 X	Chinese Horoscopes		£5.99	£
	copies of 0 340 60882 X	Dowsing		£5.99	£
	copies of 0 340 60150 7	Dream Interpretation	✓	£5.99	£
	copies of 0 340 62079 X	Feng Shui		£5.99	£
	copies of 0 340 60883 8	Gems & Crystals	✓	£5.99	£
	copies of 0 340 60625 8	Graphology		£5.99	£
	copies of 0 340 62080 3	I-Ching	✓	£5.99	£
	copies of 0 340 64805 8	Love Signs		£5.99	£
	copies of 0 340 64835 X	Meditation	✓	£5.99	£
	copies of 0 340 59551 5	Numerology		£5.99	£
	copies of 0 340 59552 3	Palmistry		£5.99	£
	copies of 0 340 67013 4	Paganism		£5.99	£
	copies of 0 340 62081 1	Runes	✓	£5.99	£
	copies of 0 340 59553 1	Star Signs	✓	£5.99	£
	copies of 0 340 59550 7	Tarot		£5.99	£
	copies of 0 340 64836 8	The Moon and You	✓	£5.99	£
	copies of 0 340 65495 3	Visualisation	✓	£5.99	£
	copies of 0 340 67014 2	Witchcraft	✓	£5.99	£
				TOTAL	£

Name ....

Address ....

....

.... Post Code ....

If you would prefer to pay by credit card, please complete:

Please debit my Visa/Access/Diner's Card/American Express (delete as appropriate) card no:

☐☐☐☐☐☐☐☐☐☐☐☐☐☐☐☐☐

Signature .... Expiry Date..

For sales in the following countries please contact:
UNITED STATES: Trafalgar Square (Vermont), Tel: 800 423 4525 (toll-free)
CANADA: General Publishing (Ontario), Tel: 445 3333
AUSTRALIA: Hodder & Stoughton (Sydney), Tel: 02 638 5299